*Hilaire Belloc*

Twayne's English Authors Series

Kinley E. Roby, Editor

*Northeastern University*

TEAS 347

HILAIRE BELLOC
(1870 – 1953)
*Courtesy of Gerald Duckworth & Co. Ltd.*
*and the Estate of H. Belloc.*

# Hilaire Belloc

## By Michael H. Markel

*Drexel University*

*Twayne Publishers* • *Boston*

*Hilaire Belloc*

Michael H. Markel

Copyright © 1982 by G.K. Hall & Company
All Rights Reserved
Published by Twayne Publishers
A Division of G.K. Hall & Company
70 Lincoln Street
Boston, Massachusetts 02111

Book Production by John Amburg
Book Design by Barbara Anderson

Printed on permanent/durable acid-free
paper and bound in The United States of
America.


**Library of Congress Cataloging in Publication Data**

Markel, Michael H.
    Hilaire Belloc.

    (Twayne's English authors series ; TEAS 347)
    Bibliography: p. 163
    Includes index.
    1. Belloc, Hilaire, 1870—1953—Criticism and
interpretation.  I. Title.  II. Series.
PR6003.E45Z77   1982     828'.91209      82-8518
ISBN 0-8057-6833-5                    AACR2

# Contents

## About the Author

Michael H. Markel is Assistant Professor of Humanities and Communications at Drexel University. He received the B.A. from Lehigh University and the M.A. and Ph.D. from The Pennsylvania State University. He has written about Shakespeare, Marvell, Lovelace, Suckling, and A. E. Housman.

# Preface

Hilaire Belloc was once as well known in England as H. G. Wells and Bernard Shaw, two of his favorite antagonists. For a period of forty years, he was a great national personality, known for his spirited attacks on the British political and economic structure and his equally spirited defense of the Catholic Church. By profession, he was a writer; by instinct, a reformer. Through his writing he attempted to warn his readers about the ways in which the English institutions methodically sabotaged their freedoms. His opinions were generally radical, sometimes frustratingly theoretical, but always interesting. And although many disagreed with what he said, they knew it to be their intellectual responsibility to listen.

Belloc's deep involvement in the important issues of his day was his attempt to bring about a restructuring of English and European society. He wanted nothing less than to recapture the simple agrarian world of the high Middle Ages. In dozens of historical studies he attempted to explain how the concept of benevolent monarchy was supplanted by corrupt republicanism. In a number of satirical novels he exposed the tactics by which businessmen and professional politicians kept themselves in power at the expense of the average citizen.

Only in some of his poems and essays and in one novel did Belloc permit himself to celebrate the eternal themes of love and mutability. Had he not been driven to write so many polemical works because of his desire for practical reform—and because of persistent financial need—he might have become a major poet. In surveying the work of a man who wrote almost as many books as this study has pages, I have tried to focus on Belloc's writings of enduring value. Accordingly, his war journalism, partisan Catholic writings, and most of his geographical studies are not discussed.

His poetry receives the greatest emphasis in this book. I have attempted to show that Belloc was a first-rate craftsman in the classical tradition of A. E. Housman. Belloc's controversial histories form the largest category of his work. Ignoring the conventions of scholarly analysis and giving free rein to his Catholic perspective, he produced highly readable and vivid accounts of the French Revolution and post-Reformation England. My analysis of the histories focuses on their appeal to the general reader. In discussing his novels, I have tried to trace the evolution of his outlook from realistic political satire to philosophical fables and farces. My treatment of Belloc's essays covers a representative sampling of his favorite modes, such as satire, comedy, and elegy. A chapter is devoted to his works of controversy, covering his political and economic theses, his study of Judaism, and his famous feud with H. G. Wells. Finally, I discuss three of his travel books, which together constitute an inclusive look at Belloc's spiritual odyssey.

A word of explanation about the structure of this study. I have chosen a generic organization because Belloc thought and worked in terms of the various genres. In addition, although the tone of his work changed over the years, the evolution of his thought was slight. I have ordered the chapters according to the sequence in which the major works in each genre were written. The poetry, for example, dominates his early years and therefore is treated first. Only the chapter on the travel books, in effect his autobiography, is taken out of sequence.

Michael H. Markel

*Drexel University*

# Acknowledgments

I would like to thank Alfred A. Knopf, Inc., for permission to quote generous selections of poety from Hilaire Belloc's *Complete Verse* (Gerald Duckworth, 1970); and Gerald Duckworth & Co., Ltd. and the Estate of H. Belloc for permission to reproduce the photograph of Belloc.

My thanks are due, too, to West Virginia University Press, which printed, in *Essays on the Literature of Mountaineering*, a version of Chapter 7.

Dr. Martha B. Montgomery, Head of the Department of Humanities-Communications, and Dean Thomas Canavan of the College of Humanities and Social Sciences at Drexel University, lightened my teaching load while I worked on this book. Mrs. Lee Endicott deserves thanks for typing the manuscript.

Dr. Kinley E. Roby of Northeastern University has been of great assistance in helping me put the book together. Dr. Stanley Weintraub of The Pennsylvania State University has provided the same expert guidance in this project that he has in most of my previous work. My biggest debt, however, is to my wife, Rita, who has made this book as good as it is. I, of course, take full responsibility for its shortcomings.

# Chronology

| 1914—1918 | Wrote war journalism for *Land and Water*. |
| 1918 | Death of son, Louis Belloc. |
| 1922 | *The Jews, The Mercy of Allah*. |
| 1923 | *Sonnets and Verse*. |
| 1925 | *The Cruise of the "Nona."* |
| 1928 | *Belinda*. |
| 1934 | *Cromwell*. |
| 1938 | *Sonnets and Verse, Monarchy*. |
| 1941 | Death of son, Peter Belloc. |
| 1953 | Hilaire Belloc died at home in Sussex. |

## Chapter One

# Life and Times

## Birth and Early Years

Hilaire Belloc was born on July 27, 1870, in the small village of La Celle St. Cloud, a few miles from Paris. A violent thunderstorm broke out a few hours before his birth, the first of two signs of the turbulence and controversy that were to mark the life of the poet, historian, essayist, novelist, journalist, and Catholic propagandist.

The more ominous sign was the outbreak of the Franco-Prussian War only a few days after Belloc's birth. The war had been expected for a few months, and the Bellocs, like most of their neighbors, were anxious about the future. When the French soldiers began to survey the hills around the village and installed a large piece of artillery in the town, the Bellocs decided to move to Paris, from which they could travel easily should the powerful Prussian army break through the French frontier.[1]

Belloc's mother, an Englishwoman born Elizabeth Parkes, opposed the move to Paris, for she believed that even if the Prussians did conquer the city and its surrounding villages, the humane and courteous soldiers would pose no threat to the French civilians.[2] Before she married Louis Belloc in 1867, Elizabeth Parkes had been a prominent political activist in England, a tireless worker for the cause of women's rights.[3] Among her friends were George Eliot, Elizabeth Barrett Browning, William Makepeace Thackeray, and Anthony Trollope.[4] Her father, Joseph Parkes, had been influential in the passage of the Reform Bill of 1832, which extended voting privileges to the English middle class. Her most famous ancestor, however, was her great-grandfather, Joseph Priestley, the scientist who discovered oxygen and is sometimes called the father of modern chemistry.

Elizabeth Parkes had met Louis Belloc when she was visiting Paris in 1866. She rented a cottage in La Celle St. Cloud, in part because

I

she liked the village, but also to meet the landlord and his wife, Hilaire and Louise Swanton Belloc. Hilaire Belloc, grandfather of the writer who was given his name, was a respected artist, and Mrs. Belloc a writer of biographies and children's books.[5] Living with the Bellocs was their son, Louis, with whom Elizabeth fell in love.

A romance between Louis Belloc and Elizabeth Parkes seemed unlikely. Elizabeth was thirty-nine years old, and Louis, a few years younger, was an invalid who for years had been unable to practice his profession of law. Neither of the two families approved of the relationship because of Louis's frail health and their different cultures. The two became engaged anyway, and even after a physician told Louis that he could never become a father and both families assumed the engagement would therefore be called off, the couple married.[6] Hilaire Belloc was their second child.

When war threatened in 1870, despite Elizabeth's objections the Bellocs packed up their belongings, their daughter, Marie, and the weeks-old infant Hilaire and took the train to Paris, where they lived for about a month. When the French government fell to Bismarck's forces on September 4, 1870, the family made plans to leave for England. They departed reluctantly on the last train from Paris; as they traveled north, they watched the French soldiers shoveling dirt onto the tracks behind the train, thus denying the occupying Prussians the French railroad network.[7]

This last-minute retreat from Paris almost certainly saved the lives of the two Belloc children, for during the winter of the Prussian occupation of Paris almost every child under three years old died of malnutrition.[8] The animals in the Paris zoo were ordered slaughtered, as were the dogs and cats and most horses. At one point during the winter, the daily ration was two ounces of bread and one ounce of horse meat.[9]

When Elizabeth and Louis returned to La Celle in the summer, her faith in the essential goodness of humanity was further shaken. Their home, and the entire village, had been reduced almost to rubble by the Prussian artillery. Worse still, the conquering troops had camped in the house and systematically pillaged it. They destroyed books and manuscripts, drew beards on the faces in the portraits, and shot bullet holes through everything else they could find. For no apparent reason, they leveled the chestnut grove near the house.[10] These were the memories of war that Hilaire Belloc was to grow up with.

The second great upheaval in his early life occurred when he was only two years old: the death of his father, due to severe sunstroke. The effect on young Hilaire was indirect; the real victim was his mother. She would not allow her husband's name to be inscribed on the cross above his grave, for the thought of seeing his name there was too much for her to bear.[11] She never did wholly break free of the melancholy and depression; years after his death she described her existence without her husband: "Ma vie est finie."[12]

## Years of Quest

At age six the precocious young Hilaire was bilingual in English and French, and writing poetry. He was also drawing sophisticated sketches and maps, a habit he continued his entire life. The family was now settled in London, and with his father's French influence gone, the boy became almost thoroughly English. A nurse employed by Mrs. Belloc called the boy Hilary, and that English pronunciation remained with him, although he never abandoned the French spelling.[13]

The family moved from London to a small town in rural Sussex when, in 1878, they lost a twenty-thousand pound inheritance through unsuccessful investments.[14] At age ten Hilaire was sent to the Oratory School, near Birmingham, run by the great Cardinal Newman. He received an excellent Catholic education and won many academic prizes, but his letters from this period are somewhat melancholy.[15] What he was to remember about the Oratory School years later was his rigorous training in the classics.

In his final letter home from school at age seventeen Belloc responded to his mother's questions about his eventual plans: "I want to live in England. In an English profession I believe I shall gain a place in English writing."[16]

A few months after writing this letter, however, Belloc left the Oratory School and declared his desire to join the French navy.[17] To accomplish this, he wanted to enroll in the College Stanislas, in Paris, which graduated many young men into the French armed forces. Neither his family nor Cardinal Newman approved of this idea, believing Hilaire to be fundamentally English by this point in his life, but the boy persisted and enrolled in the Paris college in October, 1887.[18] He lasted only one term, mostly because of the school's disciplinary code. Belloc wanted to wander the streets of Paris whenever he wished, but the regulations required that he be accompanied by an escort.[19] He felt as if he were a prisoner within the great city of Paris, and so he left the college and made his way back to England.

His next experiment, in 1888, had him living on a farm in Sussex, attempting to learn to be a land agent. Although he enjoyed the physical life on the farm, he soon tired of the routine. He wrote, in French, a satirical account of the rural life and his host couple and sent it to a friend. The couple intercepted the letter, had it translated, and promptly asked him to leave.[20]

Belloc was attempting more constructive literary efforts at this time, but his letters show the same youthful egotism that led to his problem on the farm. In one letter home, for instance, he told his mother that he was going to be more selective in sending out his verse to be published in the small journals: "I cannot write short things like 'Buzenval' to order; what I write will have my name on the bottom and I do not care to feed people with a spoon, especially if later they are to read me. I am filled with a most gigantic conceit in this respect. If I suppress which, I cannot write with any power. Conceit is the very life of all effort . . ."[21]

After a summer rowing on an Irish river and a winter working in an architect's office, Belloc at nineteen began work as a journalist.[22] His sister, Marie, had introduced him to the editor of the *Pall Mall Gazette*, to which he began to contribute reviews. Although he clearly enjoyed getting paid for his writing, he soon despised "these Rhymsters and Paragraphists and these would-be thinkers of the Reviews . . ."[23] He didn't object to their getting paid for their work; rather, he hated their willingness to write anything as long as it paid. At this point in his life he believed that a writer must be "a zealot for something," just as he himself loved "that free and happy forbearance and that perfection of Charity" that he found lacking in England.[24]

This comment shows some of the characteristic attitudes and ideas that were to define the thinking of Hilaire Belloc for the remaining sixty-three years of his life. Although necessity forced him to abandon his own code, he maintained that a writer must love his subject and be more interested in communicating an idea or impression than in creating a "literary" work. For Belloc, that idea or impression was often the need to revive the influence of the Catholic Church in England and Europe. As his life progressed and he suffered personal tragedies, his devotion to the Catholic cause became the essential mission in his life, but even at nineteen he was beginning to define his conception of the writer's devotion to the Faith.

Predominant in Belloc's mind at this point, however, was not religion but politics. His French ancestry taught him an abiding love of the ideals, if not the excesses, of the French Revolution. The rebellion against the privileged classes was to become a central concern in his historical and biographical work; as a young man in London he was acutely aware of the poverty near the Thames and, less than a mile away, "the fat city men . . . who . . . worship Law and Order."[25] Like many other young radicals in London, Belloc fervently wished for a new revolution: "it will make Kings jump like coffee beans on the roaster . . ."[26] When the great war came some quarter of a century later, it was not the one he had anticipated, nor was he the "Red-Republican" he fashioned himself at age twenty.

Belloc devoted these political energies to the first of his several publishing ventures. In 1889 he and a friend, A. H. Pollen, founded the *Paternoster*, a monthly magazine, whose goals included battling those "at war with" the common ideas of morality and those whose art makes men "morbid, tired, unhappy."[27] The *Paternoster* struggled like many other small journals and expired after six issues. Competition for the reading public was intense, and, as Belloc's sister suggests, neither her brother nor Pollen was much of a businessman.[28]

## Love

The great event of Belloc's personal life occurred at this time: he met his future wife, Elodie Hogan, a native of Napa, California. Along with a sister and her mother, Elodie was returning from a trip to Rome. Part of the reason for the trip was to help her decide whether she wanted to enter a convent or marry a young suitor in California.

The Hogans were staying in London before sailing to the United States. At tea one day at a friend's Belloc met Elodie and apparently fell in love with her immediately.

Although he was not yet twenty years old and had no steady job, he wanted to become engaged to her. She refused, thinking in part of the young man in California, but mostly about her wish—and her mother's—that she enter a religious order. She gratefully accepted Belloc's invitations to see the sights of London, but she seems to have had little interest in him at this time. Elodie and her sister stayed in London for about six weeks, during which time Belloc managed to make himself an attractive alternative to the religious life. When she and her sister returned to California, Elodie had no clear idea of what to do.[29]

As he had threatened, Belloc proceeded to follow her to the United States. To raise the money for the cheapest passage from Liverpool to New York, he borrowed from a friend and pawned all of the prizes he had won at the Oratory School, including a signed edition of the complete works of Cardinal Newman.[30] (His mother soon learned the valuable books were in a pawn shop and bought them back.)[31] Hilaire said he was going to visit their Priestley relatives in Philadelphia, and, as Belloc's biographer Robert Speaight puts it, "rather surprisingly" his mother believed him.[32]

Belloc's determination to win Elodie was much like his mother's to win Louis Belloc, but Hilaire's quest was more difficult. He arrived in New York with almost no money, then stayed with the Priestleys briefly in Philadelphia. Next, he set out for San Francisco, where the Hogans now lived. His money carried him only as far as the middle of the continent; after that he lived by his wits, sometimes winning money in card games, sometimes trading hasty sketches for food and a night's lodging, and often just walking beside the railroad tracks. A month after he arrived in New York he entered San Francisco.

Mrs. Hogan was not pleased to see the rumpled Belloc, but she didn't turn him away. He stayed only two weeks, for Elodie offered him no encouragement. When he arrived back east for his return voyage, he received a letter from her saying that she would not marry him. Writing to his mother, Belloc expressed how the letter affected him: "Elodie's refusal came today. It is very final and definite and I must accept it. I shall in all probability leave this country for England next Wednesday, May 6, getting to London on May 15. You must be a good friend to me, for I have been hit very hard indeed, harder than I thought I could be hit—and you are evidently the best friend I have."[33] Although this excerpt shows a curious mixture of manly fortitude and unchecked self-pity, the pain of Elodie's refusal was very real to Belloc, and he never forgot it.

## Triumph and Disappointment at Oxford

It was with a certain sense of relief, then, that Belloc received his draft notice from the French army. He was still a French citizen: even though he was living in England he had to go. As the son of a widow, however, he was required to serve only one year, not three.

He had his choice of which branch to serve in, and despite his family's urging him to join the cavalry (he was always an excellent horseman) he joined the artillery and was stationed at Toul, near the German border. Belloc's interest in the history of France made him proud to be one of her soldiers, but he soon found out that the life of a conscript was anything but romantic: days beginning at 5:30 in the morning or sometimes three or one, frequent twenty-hour shifts, long marches and maneuvers in the snowstorms and the August heat, the plainest of food. The physical routine did not break him, for he was hearty and muscular, yet he was bored and lonely. Although he was fluent in French, he was called "the Englishman" by the other soldiers, who must have kept their distance.[34] He was constantly writing home, asking his mother to send him journals and newspapers. Try as hard as he might, Hilaire Belloc at age twenty-one was essentially English.

When his year's service was completed, Belloc refused an offer to stay on in the army as an interpreter and came home. He continued to do some free-lance writing and published poems in small journals, but basically he had no idea what direction to pursue. His sister, Marie, after talking to a professor at Oxford, decided to raise enough money for her brother to enroll at the great university. Realizing that he would not accept money from her, she silently signed away her share of the family trust fund; Belloc learned only that "a friend" of the family was willing to finance his education at Oxford.[35]

Marie Belloc was unfamiliar with the process of gaining admittance to the university: she thought that her brother's intelligence and the money would be sufficient. But each separate college at Oxford has its own policies and requirements, and the heads of at least two turned Belloc down before Dr. Benjamin Jowett, Master of Balliol, invited the great-great-grandson of Joseph Priestley to take the entrance exam, which he passed. He matriculated at Balliol in 1893.

His career at Oxford was outstanding. Among intelligent English-men the lonely Belloc blossomed. He made lifelong friends and pursued numerous sports along with his studies. Within a year he won one of the two prestigious Brackenbury scholarships in History and was active in the famous debating society, the Oxford Union.[36] He became one of the more interesting undergraduates: a French citizen who had marched halfway across America, who had served in the French army, who held firm Catholic convictions, and who could talk about it all with great gusto and imagination.

The high point of his college career came in 1894 with his election as President of the Oxford Union. An article in a university publica-tion celebrated the occasion by calling him a man who "dares to be serious and to show it." It went on to praise his use of logical deduction and rhetoric, and, perhaps most significantly, argued that he, "almost alone of Union speakers, makes converts."[37]

Belloc achieved First Class Honours in History in 1895 and was looking forward to a fellowship, the unhurried life of a professor at Oxford. He was not chosen, the second great disappointment in his life. His intellectual achievement was undeniable; perhaps what stood in his path was his tendency to proselytize. During one of his exams for the fellowship, for example, he kept a statue of the Virgin Mary on his desk,[38] this at an institution that had traditionally barred Catho-lics from earning a degree.

Perhaps more crucial than his Catholicism was his reputation for anti-Semitism, a charge that was to haunt him the rest of his life. What crystallized this reputation was his activity during the famous Dreyfus Case. Dreyfus, a Jew and a captain in the French army, was accused of espionage. Despite his claims that the incriminating documents were forged, he was convicted of treason. Belloc foolishly repeated the anti-Semitic slogans of Dreyfus's accusers—the French army—with whom he associated himself. Biographer Speaight defines the impact of this outspoken condemnation of Dreyfus: it made the Oxford community wonder whether all of his scholarship was infected by prejudice.[39] Although most people in fact agreed with Belloc that Dreyfus was guilty, his apparent anti-Semitism likely cost him his academic career. Several years later Dreyfus was pardoned and reinstated into the French army after the real forger of the incriminating documents committed suicide, but for Belloc the damage was already done.

He could never forget the disappointment of the fellowship refusal, nor could he ever really understand it. Some forty years later he wrote to a friend, still claiming that religious prejudice—the fear of an active Catholic historian—was behind the rejection.[40] The irony of this kind of statement is powerful: as a historian Belloc was to focus on the personality and character of his subject, yet in an important sense he could never clearly see himself. On another occasion he rationalized the refusal by comparing the temptation of a career at Oxford to Homer's Sirens, sapping a man's vitality and making it difficult for him to do any important work.[41] Even though Belloc's temperament probably would have made him an ineffective Oxford don, the refusal hurt him as much as Elodie's had a few years earlier.

## Marriage and Early Writings

Elodie's refusal had not been permanent, as Belloc had imagined. Apparently they kept up some kind of correspondence during the intervening five years. Then, in October, 1895, she finally took the step she had been planning for so long and joined a convent in Maryland, but she remained only a month.[42] When she wrote to him, describing her brief attempt at the religious vocation, Belloc sailed to America, along with his mother. Lecturing on history in Philadelphia, Baltimore, and New Orleans, he made his way alone to San Francisco, where he found Elodie seriously ill, apparently the result of a nervous breakdown. She recovered in a month and consented to marry him. The ceremony took place on June 16, 1896, in Napa, California. A line from a letter Belloc wrote to his mother in Philadelphia describes what Elodie's consent meant to him: "It has brought me back from I cannot tell you what precipices of insanity and despair . . ."[43]

The young couple returned to England, where Belloc's first two books were published, both in 1896: *The Bad Child's Book of Beasts* and *Verses and Sonnets*. *The Beast Book*, as he called it, was a very successful collection of nonsense verse illustrated by his Oxford friend Basil T. Blackwood. The money it brought in was critical, for their first child was born, and Belloc was trying to support his new family with University Extension lectures, tutoring, and free-lance journalism. The other book, his serious poetry, went almost unnoticed. Because he composed poetry very slowly, it was years before he got around to publishing more of it. He needed money, so he concentrated on what he could do quickly: nonsense verse and prose.

The Bellocs still lived in Oxford, and he had not given up the idea of a history fellowship. Several were vacant, but he was rejected for each of them: his speaking and writing on Catholicism had become strident and abrasive. If a lecturer on Catholicism was not sufficiently militant, he heckled him; if a colleague made a thoughtless remark on the subject, he insulted him and refused to talk to him for several months.[44] In his mid-twenties, Belloc already demonstrated two essential characteristics: his aggressive and overbearing advocacy of Catholicism, and his inability to have any sort of professional relationship with those who held different views. Not only could he not tolerate a good number of people, but he was no longer able to persuade them of his own point of view. His arguments were often substantial and logical, but they were rarely graceful and almost never subtle. As he was able to admit years later, "I am not very much good at understanding what is going on in other people's minds."[45]

The final blow at Oxford came in 1898 when his own college, Balliol, chose another Catholic for its history fellow. Belloc sourly explained that this first Catholic to win a history fellowship at Oxford since the Reformation was chosen because he was "tame."[46] Along with stinging defeats such as this one came other setbacks that further contributed to Belloc's aggressiveness. In 1899, for instance, he inquired about a professorship at Glasgow University, but its Principal replied that his religion would prevent his election.[47] His application would not even be considered despite the fact that *Danton*, his acclaimed first history, had appeared earlier that year. He was to become a professional writer, not a professor.

In a letter he wrote when he was sixty-six years old, Belloc defined what his Oxford experience meant to him: "Oxford is for me a shrine, a memory, a tomb, and a poignant possessing grief. All would have been well if they would have received me. . . . There are places in Oxford I will not pass, lest the memories should be too violent."[48]

That was Belloc's opinion late in his life. Before the disappointment had a chance to become part of his memory, he dealt with it more constructively, by creating a prose satire about an unimaginative and thoroughly conventional fictional Oxford don. Published in 1900, *Lambkin's Remains* was actually a collection of articles Belloc had been writing for a local paper. At this point in his life he was able to maintain a healthy perspective, largely because he could see that even his painful defeats sometimes had their humorous aspects: although he was depressed by his uncertain future, "I am merry when I consider the folly, wickedness and immense complexity of the world."[49]

Belloc wrote more nonsense verse to make money, and he kept tutoring Oxford students for their exams, but by the end of the century he was devoting the bulk of his time to writing French history. His primary interest was English history, but his publisher suggested that French history would be more successful because of his name; forever penniless, he was in no position to argue.[50]

The favorable critical reception of *Danton* (1899) encouraged Belloc. Often considered his best biography, it revealed the two characteristics that were to distinguish all of his historical studies: a lively and dramatic narrative style and a disregard for the conventions of scholarly writing. Not yet thirty years old, Belloc had become an important new historian.

## The Journalist

With *Danton* and *Lambkin's Remains* behind him, Belloc and his family left the sheltered world of Oxford and moved to London. He had already been writing reviews, articles, and poetry for *The Speaker*, a London journal. Here he met G. K. Chesterton, who became a close friend. Although the two men were very different, they thought alike on many issues, especially the role of Catholicism in the modern world, and became in the public mind a single entity: Chesterbelloc.

Chesterbelloc and *The Speaker* became notorious for their unpopular stand during the Boer War (1899–1902). The Boers were descendants of eighteenth-century Dutch and French colonists living in South Africa. England acquired the territory from the Dutch in 1815 and attempted to anglicize it by making English the official language and by abolishing the Boers' practice of enslaving the native blacks. The Boers moved further north to distance themselves from the English colonists, but the discovery of gold and diamonds in the Boer territory led to tensions and, in 1895, overt military actions by the English. By 1900, the numerically superior English had won their war of imperialism, and in 1902 a peace treaty was signed. Belloc and the other writers for *The Speaker* found themselves in the small pro-Boer camp; advocating the cause of Dutchmen who kept slaves and who were killing English soldiers made Belloc appear, to many, a traitorous crank. But his argument, which history has vindicated, was that the Boers were justified in defending themselves against the imperialist English, whose expansion coincided with the discovery of valuable resources under the Boer land.

Although Belloc was never far from controversy, the early years of the new century saw some of his more serene writing. In 1900 he published *Paris*, which combined the modes of personal essay and history. Although the book concluded with the beginning of the French Revolution, it was a popular guide for English tourists going to the Paris Exposition of 1900.[51] In 1902 perhaps his greatest work, *The Path to Rome*, appeared. It was a new kind of book—a travelogue/essay/spiritual autobiography—recounting the author's adventures on a walking tour in 1901 from Toul, France, to Rome. The book sold over one hundred thousand copies and firmly established Belloc's literary reputation. Before it was published, he was known as an aggressive journalist, given to eccentric views; after its publication, he was thought of as a writer in the tradition of Sterne and Rabelais.

Belloc's personal life was peaceful at this time, too, his only problem the perennial one of poverty. A second child, a daughter, was born, and Belloc still had no regular source of income. He relied on what his books and his free-lance work would earn. On his way to Toul to embark on the march to Rome he was writing his next history, *Robespierre*, in the train, in cabarets, wherever he could sit down: the manuscript was to bring him sixty-five pounds. One journal owed him six pounds; another, seven; and the London University Extension, for which he taught, twelve.

To support his family, Belloc wrote at a tremendous rate during his thirties. He averaged better than two books a year, plus reviews, articles, and poetry, and pamphlets for Catholic organizations. In addition, he maintained a busy schedule of teaching and lecturing. But still he was short of money, and after the births of two more children, he decided to become a lawyer. He studied for the bar examination, but inexplicably retreated as soon as he saw the test. He decided, instead, on a political career, without realizing, perhaps, that being a member of Parliament would only increase his financial difficulties.

## The Uncomfortable Member of Parliament

Highly individualistic as he was, Belloc was never meant to be a party man, but he was closer in philosophy to the Liberals than to the Conservatives, so he asked the Liberal organization to help him find a constituency that needed a candidate. South Salford, near Manchester in the heart of England, was the party's choice, and although it was less than ten percent Catholic, Belloc presented himself to the voters. When asked about his religion, he ignored his party's advice by answering simply that religion was far more important to him than politics, and that should a conflict arise between the two, he would automatically sacrifice his political ideals.[52] The straightforward honesty of the response appealed to the voters: they approved his candidacy unanimously. An official candidate, Belloc now waited for an election to be called.

Meanwhile, in 1905 he contracted pleuropneumonia and almost died. The London *Times* prepared its obituary, and Elodie called a priest to her husband's bedside.[53] But he started to recover and immediately sailed to Algeria in North Africa to escape the English winter. While convalescing there, he wrote *Esto Perpetua*, a book about the history and geography of the region, to pay his expenses.

When he returned to London, he moved his household to a rented farm in Sussex, for, like his mother before him, he could not afford to live in the city.

Late in 1905 the Conservative government fell, and a general election was called. Belloc campaigned on the platform of anti-imperialism, Home Rule for Ireland, and free trade.[54] Again, he responded honestly when the voters asked him about his religion. He took a rosary out of his pocket and declared that he "tell[s] these beads" every day. "If you reject me on account of my religion, I shall thank God that He has spared me the indignity of being your representative."[55] He was greeted with wild applause. He expected to lose the election because the incumbent was a Conservative and because his opponents were arguing that Belloc was not only Catholic, but a Frenchman, too (in fact, he had become a naturalized British citizen in 1902). When the votes were tallied on January 13, 1906, Belloc had won.

The Liberal Party soon began to question the wisdom of having supported Belloc for election. The first issue on which he split from the party was the Education Bill in 1906. This Liberal-sponsored bill called for a complicated scheme that would allow schools with a certain percentage of non-Anglican children to hire teachers of that religion. Although this concept would apparently favor the Catholics—they were the only substantial non-Anglican minority—Belloc was against it because it meant that if a school had fewer than the required percentage of non-Anglican students, it would not have to employ any non-Anglican teachers. Belloc in this case was asking for the impossible; and then he was unwilling to accept a compromise that would have made the religious instruction virtually nondenominational. In effect, he was not satisfied with instruction that was inoffensive to people of his faith; he demanded instruction in that faith. This exasperated not only his fellow Liberals but his fellow Catholics as well, who saw his position as stubborn and illogical. Wearied by the incessant debates and amendments, the government finally withdrew the bill.[56]

His unexpected election to Parliament affected Belloc in several ways. It cut into his income sharply, by preventing him from delivering so many lectures and by tying him to London. And even though it earned him a higher rate when he did sell his writing, he was unable to write as much. He still averaged two full-length books a year while he served, but one wonders what he could have done if all he had had to do was write. Perhaps more important, his performance in Parliament made it public knowledge that he found it hard to compromise and get along with people. This shortcoming impeded his search for any kind of salaried position. He often lamented the fact that "my inferiors" had no trouble finding regular work.[57] Even at age thirty-six, Belloc was unable to understand his own weaknesses or what the world was interested in. He was surprised and offended when he could not find a sponsor for "a good *radical* weekly. . . . First Oxford wouldn't give me work and now . . . London won't."[58] Late in 1906, however, he was appointed literary editor of the *Morning Post*, a position he held until 1910.[59]

Before the 1907 session of Parliament opened, Belloc drew more puzzled looks after he published a letter in a Manchester newspaper demanding that his own party's funds be audited.[60] He was trying to inform the public that political funds are gained through the sale of honors, but the Liberal officials must have wondered why he did not demand an audit of the Conservative party funds.

However eccentric and distressing this kind of letter was to his Liberal colleagues, it meant little to Belloc; he saw what he considered an abuse, and so he wrote a quick letter to the paper. He claimed to be uninterested in causing a stir; certainly he never bothered to avoid one. He was probably too busy to worry about the effects of everything he wrote, for he wrote all day long. A typical day's work would include writing two newspaper essays, three or four letters, three or four thousand words of his current book, and a telegram or two. Belloc's philosophy on writing was simple: "write and write and write and then offer it for sale, just like butter."[61]

Another part of many days' work was a political speech and a paid lecture. In a letter to a friend Belloc described how he handled lecture invitations. After receiving a telegram asking whether he would talk on travel, he wrote, "I will lecture on the Proper Method of Milking a Cow, which I have never done . . . [or] . . . on the Influence of the Jesuits on Europe, or on the Influence of Europe on the Jesuits. . . . I will lecture on anything in any manner for money."[62] The traveling often fatigued Belloc, for he would frequently go on week-long excursions with some six or seven lectures, but the lecturing itself was easy for him. He never prepared a lecture in the traditional sense; his scope of knowledge was tremendous because of his varied experiences and voracious reading habits. And in general he was a magnificent speaker, largely due to his years debating at the Oxford Union. In fact, he wrote most of his articles and books by dictating them, at full speed, to a loyal secretary who tried hard to keep pace. He could quite literally speak for hours on any number of subjects. When he was done lecturing or dictating at the end of a fourteen-hour day, he would go to a friend's house and they would talk far into the night.

Except for G. K. Chesterton, most of Belloc's friends were not literary people. Belloc went about his own writing—not quietly so much as independently—without noticing those around him. He liked and respected Max Beerbohm, Aldous Huxley, and Joseph Conrad, and liked but did not respect Bernard Shaw. His least favorite writers were the world-weary aesthetes and decadents, those whose spiritual leader had been Walter Pater and whose spokesman the brilliant Oscar Wilde. To their rallying call of "Art for Art's Sake" Belloc would have replied, "Art for money's sake, and Catholicism for God's sake." A letter from 1909 defines his inability to understand his near contemporaries: "When people said that beauty thrilled them so much, it merely bored me because beauty in my experience had thrilled everybody; and when they pointed to the grotesque or the misshapen as examples of beauty, I thought it simply silly."[63] Certainly Belloc had a serious difference of opinion with the Wilde school about the nature and function of art. But, as he had done all his life when he did not like something, he remained content to not like it and made no real effort to understand it.

Belloc continued to write his own classical poetry. But he had trouble fitting it into his crowded days. Notes in the margins of some surviving manuscripts show him trying to push himself on: "this has got to be finished!" and "That's all right, but you must jog the Muse."[64] The biographer Robert Speaight suggests another possible explanation for Belloc's relatively small poetic output. His mind and heart were often troubled, even if his soul was serene, and he couldn't manipulate his poetry; it remained consistent with his mood of melancholy and despair, and thus inconsistent with his avowed Catholicism.[65]

When Belloc's position as literary editor of the *Morning Post* ended in 1910, he lost his only regular income. Belloc's explanation for his leaving was that the paper was trying to print fewer of his articles and thereby reduce his salary. He claimed that he told the editor that as long as he could maintain his annual salary of about five hundred pounds and keep his title, he would be willing to write more for the paper. Belloc argued that with his growing reputation he was getting more lucrative offers for his articles individually than the paper was paying him. The editor accepted his resignation. But one of the editor's letters to Belloc suggests that the problem was more personal than professional: after apologizing for shouting at him the other day, the editor begged him to try not to "stand in my door and wag a finger at me when I am engaged on private . . . business."[66] Belloc was oblivious to even the basics of business protocol.

## "To chuck Westminster"

This contentiousness and independence marked Belloc's actions in that same year, 1910, when another general election was called. His experience in the House of Commons had convinced him that the forces of deceit and hypocrisy would prevent any real progress toward a more just society; in fact, for several reasons he no longer wished to serve in Parliament: "Every day . . . makes me more determined to chuck Westminster; it is too low for words. The position is ridiculous and the expense is damnable. . . . it cuts into my life, interferes with my earnings, and separates me from my home—all three irritating."[67] In this election, unlike the one in 1906, he ran without the support of the Liberal Party. His platform was simple: to make the rich less rich and the poor less poor.[68] He was reelected, although his margin of victory was smaller than it had been in 1906. He received only five hundred of the eight hundred Catholic votes, probably because of his stubborn refusal to compromise on the Education Bill. In addition, many of the moneyed interests in his district switched to the Conservatives on hearing his "tax the rich" speeches.

Belloc's first project after his reelection was to help the other radicals reform the voting practices that virtually gave the House of Lords veto power over any bill passed by the Commons. This reform was a difficult undertaking, for it was generally believed that the king would create as many peerages as necessary to pack the House of Lords and thus maintain the status quo. The Civil War in the seventeenth century effectively determined that Parliament, not the monarch, ruled England, but Belloc and his colleagues now wanted to know who ruled Parliament.

The issue of electoral reform within Parliament and in the general elections as well led to a crisis, and another election was called in 1910, the only time the English voted twice in the same year. This time Belloc refused to run. He wrote to a colleague who asked him to change his mind, responding that when "realities" returned to politics he would return.[69] He never did. His final speech to Parliament, a scathing indictment of the party system, was attended by only some twenty or thirty members.

Belloc and Cecil Chesterton, Gilbert's brother, published in 1911 *The Party System*, which expanded and elaborated the Parliament speech. The thesis of the book is that the party system, which was intended to encourage democracy by fostering the adversary relationship between the two major parties, was a sham, a means of disguising collusion among the leaders of both factions. In 1912 the Marconi scandal justified, in part at least, the charges contained in the book. The Marconi Company was a communications corporation with a subsidiary in the United States. In 1911 the company had been granted by Parliament a monopoly contract to build telegraph stations in Great Britain. Belloc and Cecil Chesterton, who were then publishing a journal called the *New Witness*, were suspicious of the contract, for they learned that the Marconi Company was run by a notoriously unsuccessful financier, a man named Isaacs who had declared bankruptcy in some twenty previous business ventures.[70] The *New Witness* learned that David Lloyd George, then finance minister of the ruling Liberal Party and later prime minister, had invested heavily in the American Marconi Company and seen the market value of the stock jump from fourteen to one hundred shillings. Lloyd George was never formally punished for his conflict of interest; when the Conservatives in the House of Commons attempted to censure "certain of its Ministers" for their transactions and their lack of candor in responding to inquiries about the scandal, the motion was defeated.[71]

Belloc's next public opponent was Ramsay MacDonald, a socialist who after World War I was to become the Labour Party's prime minister. MacDonald was one of the architects of the modern English welfare state. Although MacDonald's enemies and his were the same, Belloc thought that the citizens risked endangering too much of their liberty by creating a governing class that might be even more unrepresentative than the existing parliamentary class. *The Servile State* (1912) is Belloc's prophetic account of how the English surrendered more and more of their personal freedom in the creation of the welfare state.

## The Years of Tragedy

Having quit Parliament, Belloc entered a period of relative tranquillity. He lived with his family at King's Land, their rambling house in Sussex, and wrote prolifically. His still-respected history of the French Revolution, plus a historical novel about the same period, a satirical novel, and a travel book about Sussex—all were produced in the prewar years. Belloc's theory of writing remained the same: "If they won't buy one kind of book, then I write another. . ."[72] Except for the traveling he did to research battle sites for his books, he was home most of the time and developed many close friends with whom he and his wife visited often.

But these peaceful few years were not to last. In 1914 Elodie died, and it almost destroyed Belloc. At the age of only forty-three, he became an old man. Part of his distress was guilt, the feeling that Elodie had always been of delicate health, and that his inability to get a secure teaching position at Oxford kept him from providing the stable home that she required. He felt, too, that his own active life, symbolized by his march to Rome, was essentially selfish and that he should have stayed home more. None of his friends understood or condoned this guilt, but Belloc persisted despite their efforts to help him deal with his loss. It is no exaggeration to say that for several months after Elodie's death, he was close to suicidal: he expressed to a close friend an "increasing doubt whether I can live my life."[73] His faith prevented his acting on such thoughts, of course. His life, in fact, was but half done; he was to live thirty-nine more years.

The death of Elodie signaled only the beginning of what were probably Belloc's most difficult years. Ironically, the one bright spot for him was that World War I enabled him to earn fame and money as a military analyst for a new journal, *Land and Water*. He was particularly well suited for this position because of his intimate knowledge of the terrain of Europe and his expertise in European history, especially military history. For a reading public that expected the English troops to march into Berlin in a few months, his articles provided a useful measure of reality; he was unafraid to praise the military accomplishments of the Germans when they deserved it. His articles were long—often seven or eight thousand words—and they reached one hundred thousand readers.[74] Belloc himself became something of a celebrity for the first time in his life. Although he was sometimes criticized and parodied for his occasionally inaccurate predictions, the British public came to rely on him to explain how the war was progressing. His public speaking increased, to more than one lecture a day, and with it his income.

But along with the excitement of conferring with the most important military leaders, including Marshal Foch of France and General Pershing of the United States, came the inevitable tragedies of war. Belloc lost many close friends, including his closest, Cecil Chesterton. In 1917 Louis, Belloc's eldest son, was gassed as an infantryman in France.[75] While recovering in England, he transferred into the flying corps. On a mission in 1918, just weeks before the end of the war, his plane was lost. His body was never recovered. In a letter to a friend Hilaire Belloc talked about his memories of his son, "especially his early childhood and the days before any disasters came."[76]

## The Tired Fighter

The deaths of his friends, his wife, and then his son transformed Belloc. Despite his still-frenetic schedule of lectures, articles, and books of all kinds, he seemed to withdraw from the world. He devoted more and more of his time to religious writings. He continued to attack his old enemies—the forces of money and corrupt power—but his reading public shrank, for everyone who was interested already knew what he had to say. Whereas before the war he argued to defeat his opponents, now he argued to encourage his allies. He was no longer an effective spokesman for political, social, or religious ideas.

As the literary world changed, Belloc seemed more of an anachronism. His favorite contemporary poet was the now-unknown Ruth Pitter. Of the novelists, he admired his friend Maurice Baring, a satirist, and P. G. Wodehouse, the comic genius whose novels are set in a hazily imprecise pre-war England. As he grew older, he read fewer contemporary works, for "language is forgotten." Literature had become foolish and obscene. "For whom should any man now write? What ears remain to hear?"[77] Belloc read and reread the English classics, and Virgil, Catullus, and Homer. When he was thirty, Belloc could not understand what people were writing; when he was fifty, he no longer tried.

It is easy to overstate Belloc's separateness from the writers of his day. When we think back to the literature of the early 1920s in England, we think of T. S. Eliot's *The Waste Land* because historical hindsight has enabled us to focus on what was truly new. But in 1922 the publication of the poem was a major event for only a relatively few writers and even fewer readers. Belloc, like most of his contemporaries, was simply reading something else at the time; very likely, he did not see the poem at all.

It is also easy to overstate the melancholy of Belloc's postwar years. His spirit had been broken, it is true, but he never lost his extraordinary ability to laugh at himself, for he believed in "the great lifebuoy of humour, which is a sort of sister or companion-aid to the Faith."[78] He laughed at his appearance: when he saw a portrait of himself painted by James Gunn, he noted that it made him look like "a powerful gorilla with a grievance: which I believe is a frequent aspect."[79] He laughed at his behavior: when he was a guest at a friend's house, he felt obliged to repay his host "with excellent buffoonery and jest."[80] He laughed at his letters, full of "nothingness, emptiness, vanity and vexation of spirit . . . repetition, vacuity . . . and every synonym for the supremely inane."[81] And he laughed at his writing: after correcting the proofs of one of his books, he remarked, ". . . all shall be ready for the accursed printer and he shall print a ton of the book which none shall buy, I hope, for its dullness passes belief. It has earned me all the money it ever will and may now go and be burnt in a bonfire by green devils for all I care."[82]

Belloc began to receive public recognition relatively early in his life. In 1916 C. Creighton Mandell and Edward Shanks wrote a flattering evaluation of him. Belloc's favorite comment from the book was that he was the best writer of English prose since Dryden. In 1920 he received an honorary Doctor of Law degree from Glasgow University, the school which would not accept his application for a teaching position a quarter century before. He was also recognized by several European governments for his war journalism. He generally disliked awards because he wanted to remain independent of any organization's control or influence. For this reason, he once refused an honor offered by the Pope, for he did not want to become an "official Catholic." The honor he was most excited about came from Oxford, the university whose rejection had forced him to become a professional writer. He was invited to speak on translation for Oxford's Taylorian lecture series in 1931. His lecture was published, and he always remained proud of it.

In the 1930s Belloc continued to write, but he stayed home at King's Land more than he ever had before. His chief joy was watching his grandchildren grow up; his sorrow was the memory of his wife and son. In addition, he had more money problems, for his increasing age limited the number of lectures he could give. When World War II came, he wrote more analyses of the fighting, but this time he was not as influential as he had been twenty-five years before. He was thought of as Belloc, the Catholic who had written about World War I. When Paris fell to the Germans, as it had when Belloc was just an infant, he thought he could not be hurt anymore.

He was wrong. In 1941, his son Peter, a marine stationed in Scotland, contracted pneumonia and died. He was buried next to his mother. Belloc's health began to fail. He himself contracted pneumonia and suffered severe headaches and insomnia. His eyesight weakened, and he couldn't read as much as he wanted. His memory diminished, and sometimes he confused his sons whom the two wars had taken from him. As he had described himself a few years earlier, "My strength is running out, like sawdust out of a worn doll."[83]

His death came in 1953. He apparently lost consciousness while gazing at the fireplace in his living room. His daughter Eleanor and her husband heard him fall; they found him lying near the fire, his coat smoldering. He was not badly burned, but he slipped in and out of consciousness. He received the Last Sacraments and three days later died, with a look of calm and peace in his eyes.

## Chapter Two
# The Poetry

During a writing career of more than forty-five years, Hilaire Belloc turned out almost one hundred and fifty prose works. With only a handful of exceptions, writing these books was an enormous chore for him, what one commentator calls his "sad campaign for a livelihood."[1] Belloc's aggressive and domineering personality prevented him from long remaining anyone's employee, so he turned his antipathy for socialists, atheists, and Darwinians into a lifelong vocation.

But Belloc's real love remained his poetry. What he wished to be remembered for is collected in a slim volume called *Complete Verse*.[2] Had circumstances been otherwise, he probably would have written ten volumes of poetry and very little else. Whereas the subject of his prose was the struggle of men in the world, their attempt to create a set of reasonable and just institutions that would allow them to lead civilized lives, the subject of his poetry was the perennial theme of man's struggle against his mortality. Belloc put into prose what he wanted the world to hear; he saved for his poetry what he *had* to say.

In addition to his serious poetry, Belloc wrote several books of light verse, most of which is collected today under the title *Cautionary Verses*. His first book of light verse, *The Bad Child's Book of Beasts*, appeared the same year as his first collection of serious poems and, much to his delight, sold briskly. Then twenty-six years old, and with a family, a prestigious First Honours in History from Oxford, and no prospects for a job, Belloc decided the serious poems would have to wait, at least for a while.

## The Light Verse

The nineteenth century in England was the great period of light verse, or what is sometimes called nonsense verse. Perhaps as a reaction to the seriousness and solemnity of Victorian advice-books for children, the writers of light verse portrayed a world in which children, unencumbered by the restrictions of "civilized" behavior, romped freely through a world bounded only by their own imaginations. The two most famous writers of light verse were Edward Lear (1812—1888) and Charles Lutwidge Dodgson (1832—1898), who is known today as Lewis Carroll.

Lear, a landscape painter by profession, popularized the short verse form known as the limerick:

> There was an Old Man with a beard, .
> Who said, "It is just as I feared!—
> Two Owls and a Hen,
> Four Larks and a Wren,
> Have all built their nests in my beard!"[3]

Lewis Carroll, a minor church official and mathematics professor at Oxford, wrote mathematics books under his real name and children's books under his pseudonym. Best remembered today as the author of *Alice's Adventures in Wonderland* (1865) and its sequel, *Through the Looking-Glass* (1871), Carroll is known for his creation of nonsense words in the poems contained within the two famous books. "Jabberwocky," in *Through The Looking-Glass*, is the prime example:

> 'Twas brillig, and the slithy toves
> Did gyre and gimble in the wabe:
> All mimsy were the borogoves,
> And the mome raths outgrabe.          (11.1—4)[4]

Although Belloc is often linked with Lear and Carroll as the third master of nonsense verse, he seems to have been largely indifferent to both of them. The limerick form appears in several of Belloc's letters to friends—he could apparently toss them off effortlessly—but it doesn't appear in any of his published verse. And Belloc seems to have been even less impressed by Carroll's nonsense verse. In fact, he was almost alone among his countrymen in not thinking *Alice's Adventures in Wonderland* a masterpiece. He described it as full of "the humour which is founded upon folly" and thus worthwhile but inferior to "the wit that is founded upon wisdom." He went on to predict—wildly incorrectly, as it has turned out—that the fame of *Alice* would not outlive the insular and protected garden of the Victorian period.[5]

Belloc remained unmoved by Lear and Carroll because he was not principally interested in writing for children. Even though the titles of his light verse collections—such as *The Bad Child's Book of Beasts* and *More Beasts (for Worse Children)*—appear at first glance to be intended for children, the adjectives "bad" and "worse" clearly suggest an adult perspective. Unlike Lear and Carroll, Belloc never tried to assume the viewpoint of the child, and there is very little childlike delight in any of the cautionary tales. Instead, Belloc wrote from the perspective of the stern parent lecturing children on the ghastly consequences of their improper behavior. Belloc achieved his humor by overstating the perils. Most of the bad children in his books die a horrible death: several are eaten by wild animals, one dies in an explosion caused in part by his own carelessness, and another succumbs because he ate too much string. Those lucky children who do not die suffer other unkind fates. Maria, for instance, constantly made funny faces. One day, "Her features took their final mould / In shapes that made your blood run cold . . ." Her sad story is suggested by the title of the poem: "Maria Who Made Faces and a Deplorable Marriage." Unlike Lear and Carroll, whose strategy was to bridge the gulf between adults and children, Belloc startled his readers by exaggerating that gulf. Belloc's view of children did not look backward to the Victorian nonsense poets, but forward to the films of W. C. Fields.

*The Bad Child's Book of Beasts* (1896) was the first appearance of Belloc's irascible narrator, who innocently announces his intentions in an introduction:

> I call you bad, my little child,
>    Upon the title page,
> Because a manner rude and wild
>    Is common at your age.
>
> The Moral of this priceless work
>    (If rightly understood)
> Will make you—from a little Turk—
>    Unnaturally good.                                                    (235)[6]

But the real personality of the narrator soon emerges. In "The Lion" he warns little children to beware:

> The Lion, the Lion, he dwells in the waste,
> He has a big head and a very small waist;
> But his shoulders are stark, and his jaws they are grim,
> And a good little child will not play with him. (236)

The next poem is "The Tiger":

> The Tiger on the other hand, is kittenish and mild,
> He makes a pretty playfellow for any little child;
> And mothers of large families (who claim to common sense)
> Will find a Tiger well repay the trouble and expense. (237)

Enhancing Belloc's humor are the drawings by his friend Basil T. Blackwood that accompany the text. "The Lion" is printed around a sketch of a terrified child gazing at the ferocious animal rearing on its hind legs before him. "The Tiger" has two sketches: in the first, a hungry-looking tiger is approaching a smiling toddler. In the second, the tiger is walking away, licking its lips. This was one of Belloc's strategies in the book: the words express the seemingly innocent advice; the drawings portray the narrator's—and the reader's—real thoughts.

This kind of macabre humor obviously is not intended for the average child. The parents are the real audience, as several other verses in the collection make clear. "The Marmozet" and "The Big Baboon" gave Belloc a chance to have a little fun with the evolutionists, with whom he was constantly quarreling, while satirizing the poverty of the modern spirit. The drawing accompanying "The Marmozet" shows three figures: a statue of a burly caveman wearing an animal pelt and carrying a club, an anemic-looking young man perspiring as he pedals his bicycle, and a marmozet casting a scornful eye on the young man.

The four-line poem makes the point:

> The species Man and Marmozet
> Are intimately linked;
> The Marmozet survives as yet,
> But Men are all extinct. (238)

"The Big Baboon" focuses Belloc's satire a little more:

> The Big Baboon is found upon
>     The plains of Cariboo:
> He goes about with nothing on
>     (A shocking thing to do).
>
> But if he dressed respectably
>     And let his whiskers grow,
> How like this Big Baboon would be
>     To Mister So-and-so!                              (239)

The drawings that go with this poem show a happy baboon in the wild, a baboon gazing at a pretentiously dressed African, a baboon gazing into a mirror while his valet helps him on with his coat, and finally several baboons walking happily down a city street, outfitted with luxurious overcoats, fashionable hats, and canes.

Some of the verses in *The Bad Child's Book of Beasts* are funny without being violent or satirical, and many of the drawings are innocently clever, but for the most part Belloc was writing in the tradition of Jonathan Swift and Mark Twain, not Lear and Carroll. Belloc chose animals for his subject not because every child likes to read about them, but because they are strong, self-sufficient, and unaffected. Belloc accepted them as creatures that know what they are, never aspire to be anything else, and never are needlessly cruel. In this way they serve as a perfect contrast to the foolish and vain species called Man. Belloc's book of nonsense verse, reminiscent of Swift's parable of the Yahoos and the Houyhnhnms in Part IV of *Gulliver's Travels*, turns the hierarchy of nature upside down. Published in Oxford, *The Bad Child's Book of Beasts* sold out in four days. A second printing began immediately, and the author arranged for publication in the United States.[7] The critics were very enthusiastic, but, as biographer Speaight remarks, they usually failed to see that the comic verse was not really nonsense.[8]

The critics also applauded *More Beasts (for Worse Children)* (1897), which Belloc published quickly to capitalize on the success of the earlier book. Its plan is the same, but on the whole the humor is forced. Several of the verses are clever. "The Microbe," for example, pokes fun at scientists who describe fantastic microscopic organisms they have never seen. "Oh! let us never, never doubt / What nobody is sure about!" intones the narrator solemnly (246). But the violence and cruelty of many of the verses is gratuitous: the woman who is devoured by a python in this book "died, because she never knew / Those simple little rules and few" about how to care for it (242). Her fate is neither humorous nor revealing.

Belloc found his mark again the next year with *The Modern Traveller* (1898), a satirical parable about imperialism. His criticism of the British role in the struggle with the Boers in South Africa was already taking shape; despite its clever verse and Blackwood's drawings, *The Modern Traveller* was obviously intended for adults, not children.

The poem describes how the narrator and two friends—Commander Sin and Captain Blood—travel to Africa to establish the Libyan Association "whose purpose is to combine 'Profit and Piety.'" Recently returned from Africa and looking over the page proofs of his memoirs, the narrator invites a reporter from the *Daily Menace* over for an exclusive article on his expedition. The explorer has plenty of pencils ready for the reporter, because the story is going to be a long one,

> Of how we struggled to the coast,
> And lost our ammunition;
> How we retreated, side by side;
> And how, like Englishmen, we died.          (165)

He begins by introducing Henry Sin:

> Untaught (for what our times require),
> Lazy, and something of a liar,
>    He had a foolish way
> Of always swearing (more or less);
>
>    And, lastly, let us say
> A little slovenly in dress,
> A trifle prone to drunkenness;
> A gambler also to excess,
>    And never known to pay.          (166–67)

In short, he was "A man Bohemian as could be— / But really vicious? Oh, no!" (167). The other hero of the expedition, William Blood,

while equally unsavory, was more at home in the modern world. He
was:

> A sort of modern Buccaneer,
> Commercial and refined.
> Like all great men, his chief affairs
> Were buying stocks and selling shares.
> He occupied his mind
> In buying them by day from men
> Who needed ready cash, and then
> At evening selling them again
> To those with whom he dined.                              (171)

When the narrator and his two partners arrive in Africa, they enlist
an accomplice, the Lord Chief Justice of Liberia, who gives them
"good advice / Concerning Labour and its Price":

> "In dealing wid de Native Scum,
> Yo' cannot pick an' choose;
> Yo' hab to promise um a sum
> Ob wages, paid in Cloth and Rum.
> But, Lordy! that's a ruse!
> Yo' get yo' well on de Adventure,
> And change de wages to Indenture."                      (183–84)

A brief mutiny results—"We shot and hanged a few, and then /
The rest became devoted men"—but soon the three adventurers find
the land they wish to develop. The narrator describes Blood's triumphant
pose:

> Beneath his feet there stank
> A swamp immeasurably wide,
> Wherein a kind of fœtid tide
> Rose rhythmical and sank,
> Brackish and pestilent with weeds
> And absolutely useless reeds . . .
>
> . . . . . . . . . . . . . . . . . . .
> With arms that welcome and rejoice,
> We heard him gasping, in a voice
> By strong emotion rendered harsh:

> "That Marsh—that Admirable Marsh!"
> The Tears of Avarice that rise
> In purely visionary eyes
> Were rolling down his nose.                    (186–87)

The development of Eldorado, as Blood christens it, is thwarted. After a confrontation with an international commission against imperialism, which concludes that they are too mad to cause any harm, the three are finally captured by a native tribe. Captain Blood is chopped up and sold by the slice ("Well, every man has got his price") and Commander Sin finds himself floating in a large kettle ("My dear companion making soup"). The narrator endures so well under incredible torture that the tribesmen finally decide he must be a god and release him. His final words to the reporter are that Sin and Blood "Would swear to all that I have said, / Were they alive; / but they are dead!" (204)

*The Modern Traveller*, like Belloc's two previous books of light verse, was very popular with the public, but it received some unenthusiastic reviews in newspapers, probably because of the satirical portrait of *The Daily Menace*. Sir Arthur Quiller-Couch explained the critical reaction by noting the link between the newspapers and imperialism: since the newspapers had been championing the cause of imperialism, they could not be expected to review fairly a book that criticizes it.[9] The outbreak of the Boer War was in fact the most revealing comment on the book. Belloc in *The Modern Traveller* had shown that light verse could be the vehicle for serious satire without losing its popular appeal.

Belloc appreciated Quiller-Couch's praise, but his financial situation left him no leisure to savor it. Most of his time was being devoted to his first serious prose work, a full-length biography of the French Revolutionary figure Danton that could not hope to bring in much. So Belloc wrote *A Moral Alphabet* (1899). The alphabet format, in which each letter introduces a short verse, gave him a ready-made structure for verses on various subjects; unlike the *Beast* collections or *The Modern Traveller*, an alphabet book needs no unifying theme.

Signs of hasty composition are apparent in *A Moral Alphabet*, but the book is interesting in that it reveals Belloc's awareness of his

audience and his growing self-confidence. Four of the twenty-six
rhymes refer directly to this or one of his other books. "A," for
instance, "stands for Archibald who told no lies, / And got this lovely
volume for a prize." When he comes to the nemesis of all alphabet
rhymsters, X, Belloc effortlessly turns the situation to his advantage:

> No reasonable little Child expects
> A Grown-up Man to make a rhyme on X.
> MORAL
> *These verses teach a clever child to find*
> *Excuse for doing all that he's inclined.*                  (258)

*A Moral Alphabet* marks the end of the first phase of Belloc's
professional literary career. With the coming of the new century he
turned to more substantial formats; he had already proven himself a
reigning master of comic verse in English. Between 1900 and 1905 he
produced, among other works, a second biography, two prose satires,
a book of literary criticism, a translation, a novel, and several travel
books.

In 1907 Hilaire Belloc, member of Parliament, must have sensed
that the public was ready for another book of light verse. *Cautionary
Tales for Children* follows in the tradition of his first *Beast* book, but it
shows a new direction in Belloc's thinking. Almost all of the children
in this collection who pay so dearly for their misdeeds belong to the
upper class. The title of one verse, "Godolphin Horne, Who was
cursed with the Sin of Pride, and Became a Boot-Black," is representative of Belloc's new interest in satirizing the rigid class system of
England. His characteristic mask in this book is that of the defender
of the class system, but occasionally the real author peeks out and
winks at his readers. One example is "Algernon, Who played with a
Loaded Gun, and, on missing his Sister, was reprimanded by his
Father." The most subtle verse is the final one, "Charles Augustus
Fortescue, Who always Did what was Right, and so accumulated an
Immense Fortune." Here Belloc takes particular advantage of Blackwood's drawings by making one statement with words and another
with pictures. The verse describes how this perfect child sailed
through life successfully,

> And long before his Fortieth Year
> Had wedded Fifi, Only Child
> Of Bunyan, First Lord Aberfylde.
> He thus became immensely Rich,
> And built the Splendid Mansion which
> Is called *"The Cedars, Muswell Hill,"*
> Where he resides in Affluence still,
> To show what Everybody might
> Become by SIMPLY DOING RIGHT.            (271)

The drawing accompanying this idyllic tale, however, shows the groom with a slightly pained expression on his face as he gazes at his decidedly unattractive bride, Fifi. Thus, Belloc's final suggestion for the best way to punish the indolent rich of England is simply to let them go about their own business unmolested. *Cautionary Tales for Children* was successful in part because a popular singer, Clara Butt, performed the verses in concert throughout England.[10]

Belloc's unorthodox parliamentary career kept him in the public eye. Frequently squabbling with his own party, he became known as something of a national eccentric, with a reputation apart from his literary renown. Just as nobody was surprised when he decided not to stand for reelection in 1910, nobody was surprised when in 1911 he published *More Peers*, a collection of cautionary verses for adults. One verse describes the unfortunate plight of a physician whose patient, a Lord Roehampton, dies without leaving enough to pay the medical fee. The furious doctor storms away when he learns this tragic news, "And ever since, as I am told, / Gets it beforehand; and in gold" (209). Another lord, Henry Chase, wins a libel suit against *The Daily Howl*, "But, as the damages were small, / He gave them to a Hospital" (209).

A Lord Finchley learns that excessive thrift has its penalties:

> Lord Finchley tried to mend the Electric Light
> Himself. It struck him dead: And serve him right!
> It is the business of the wealthy man
> To give employment to the artisan.            (210)

The highlight of *More Peers* is a story that never gets told:

> Lord Heygate had a troubled face,
> His furniture was commonplace—
> The sort of Peer who well might pass
> For someone of the middle class.
> I do not think you want to hear
> About this unimportant Peer,
> So let us leave him to discourse
> About Lord Epsom and his horse.                    (210)

Nineteen years were to pass before Belloc got around to *New Cautionary Tales* (1930), published near the end of his long career. This collection is tired, partly because Belloc was then sixty years old, but mostly because he feared that the good fight against the forces of privilege had been lost. He could not escape the realization that fifty years of struggle and one hundred and fifty books had not changed the world. One verse tells the story of how young John loses his inheritance when he tosses a stone that hits his wealthy uncle William. The old man calls to his nurse, Miss Charming,

> "Go, get my Ink-pot and my Quill,
> My Blotter and my Famous Will."
> Miss Charming flew as though on wings
> To fetch these necessary things,
> And Uncle William ran his pen
> Through "well-beloved John," and then
> Proceeded, in the place of same,
> To substitute Miss Charming's name:
> Who now resides in Portman Square
> And is accepted everywhere.                        (281)

Belloc's last book of comic verse, *Ladies and Gentlemen*, was published two years later, in 1932. It was quite obviously the work of a weary man who no longer felt that the foibles of society were a thoroughly suitable subject for humorous verse. "The Garden Party," the opening verse, describes an affair attended by "the Rich," "the Poor," and "the People in Between":

> For the hoary social curse
> Gets hoarier and hoarier,

And it stinks a trifle worse
Than in the days of Queen Victoria . . .                                 (219)

The verse concludes with a reference to the fate of an earlier corrupt civilization: "And the flood destroyed them all." The final verse in the collection, "The Example," is a parable of two modern types. The man is a miserable agnostic whose only joy is to read the books written by the prophets of doom. The woman leads a life of mindless intemperance:

The Christians, a declining band,
Would point with monitory hand
To Henderson his desperation,
To Mary Lunn her dissipation,
And often mutter, "Mark my words!
Something will happen to those birds!"                          (227)

Mary Lunn dies, "not before / Becoming an appalling bore," and Henderson is "suffering from paralysis." *"The moral is ( it is indeed!) / You mustn't monkey with the Creed"* (227). Appropriately enough, Belloc's last book of comic verse concludes with a deadly serious joke.

The comic verse, except for *The Modern Traveller*, was collected under the title *Cautionary Verses* in 1940. The critical reception was highly enthusiastic. The *New Yorker*, for example, called *Cautionary Verses* "a grand omnibus."[11] The collection remains Belloc's most popular single volume. An ironic reminder of the extent to which the satirical element in Belloc's comic verse has remained unrecognized is the fact that *Cautionary Verses* is generally catalogued among the children's books in the library. Taken together, the comic verse is a remarkable achievement. Belloc wrote too much of it, as he did of everything, but the best represents the extraordinary diversity of his imagination, which could combine pure nonsense of the highest quality and serious political and social satire. Perhaps the best insight into the origins of the comic verse is provided by Belloc himself in a poem he originally published in 1910 but which serves as an epigraph to *Cautionary Verses*. The poem, which begins "Child! do not throw this book about," ends with this stanza:

And when your prayers complete the day,
Darling, your little tiny hands
Were also made, I think, to pray
For men that lose their fairylands.                    (63)

The comic verse is of course very funny, but behind the laughter is the
sadness of an idealistic man in a real world.

### The Serious Verse

In one of his comic verses Belloc wrote a couplet, "Upon the
mansion's ample door, / To which he wades through heaps of
Straw . . ." and added a footnote: "This is the first and only time /
That I have used this sort of Rhyme" (208−9). In his comic verse he
was scrupulous about following the technical conventions, including
such matters as the crispness of the end rhymes. He once wrote that
comic verse "has nothing to sustain it save its own excellence of
construction, . . . those who have attempted it [find] that no kind
of verse needs more the careful and repeated attention of the arti-
ficer."[12] This is surely overstatement, for the rate at which he produced his comic verse would have made such refinement and polish-
ing impossible. However, the remark suggests the importance Belloc
placed on "the excellence of construction" in all of his verse.

In his relatively few serious poems, in particular, he allowed
himself the luxury of slow and careful construction, for in no other
kind of writing would he speak so candidly. Almost everything else
he wrote was intended to pay the bills. But in his serious poems he
expressed his essence, the melancholy and even the despair that tested
his Catholic faith. While the rest of Belloc's massive output contains
the record of his many opinions, the serious poetry is his purest
literary expression.

Belloc's poetic principles were classical. He deplored the contemporary trends in poetry whose origins he saw in the tenets of the
Romantics of a century earlier. He insisted that "the greatest verse
does not proceed immediately from the strongest feeling. The greatest verse calls up the strongest emotion in the reader, but in the writer
it is a distillation, not a cry."[13]

Thus, Belloc dispensed with Wordsworth's theory that poetry is born of "emotion recollected in tranquility" and with the rest of what he saw as "the romantic extravagance, the search for violent sensation, . . . the loss of measure . . ."[14] The rest of the nineteenth century was for Belloc further decay. In a grouchy mood once he wrote to a friend expressing a desire to write a series called "Twelve Great Eunuchs of the Victorian Period."[15] He reserved his most caustic comments, however, for the modern poets. One poet, "spared to middle age in spite of the wrath of God," Belloc called "famous for that he could neither scan nor rhyme—let alone think or feel."[16] And modern English lyric poetry was mere "chopped up prose."[17]

Fairly early in his life Belloc gave up trying to endure modern poetry. Except for the books written by his friends, he read little but the Latin and Greek classics in their original languages. His poetic principles are defined clearly in his book on Milton, whom he considered the last major classical poet in English:

He felt to his marrow the creative force of restraint, proportion, unity—and that is the classic . . . Rule and its authority invigorated the powers of man as pruning will a tree, as levees a pouring river. Diversity without extravagance, movement which could be rhythmic because it knew boundaries and measure, permanence through order, these were, and may again be, the inestimable fruits of the classical spirit.[18]

To the opinion that the classical style was tired, Belloc responded that "those whose energy is too abundant seek for themselves by an instinct the necessary confines without which such energy is wasted,"[19] and that "energy alone can dare to be classical."[20]

Despite his many comments on the necessity of classical restraint, Belloc did not believe that great poetry was merely the result of regular rhythms and rhymes. Like the Romantics he scorned, he felt that a poet is more than a craftsman. Just as the Romantics spoke of the divine inspiration for which they served as a vehicle, Belloc wrote that "something divine is revealed in the poetic speech, not through the poet's will but through some superior will using the poet for its purpose. It is the afflatus of the God. . . .[t]he seed of Poetry floats in from elsewhere. It is not of this world."[21] His definition of poetic

inspiration is thus explicitly theistic—god-oriented—whereas the
Romantics were more likely to think of poetry as a revelation of the
god in Man. Basically, the difference is a matter of terminology and
external beliefs, not of essentials. But Belloc was adamant in his views
on poetic form, and so he went his own unpopular way during the
years of poetic upheaval and innovation.

Belloc's respect for the classical conception of poetry is immediately apparent in his first volume of poetry, *Verses and Sonnets* (1896).
Establishing a pattern that he was to follow in all of his books of
poetry, Belloc arranged his work according to genre: sonnets, songs,
epigrams, and satires. Like the ancients, he believed that poetry is a
deliberate and self-conscious utterance and that an idea or emotion has
to be expressed in an appropriate genre to achieve its meaning.

Belloc's concern for the plight of the poor, for example, is expressed
in two poems, one a satire and one a sonnet. "The Justice of the
Peace," the satire, is a scathing dramatic monologue that begins with
this stanza:

> Distinguish carefully between these two,
>     This thing is yours, that other thing is mine.
> You have a shirt, a brimless hat, a shoe
>     And half a coat. I am the Lord benign
> Of fifty hundred acres of fat land
> To which I have a right. You understand?                    (147)

In his sonnet on the same subject, "The Poor of London," Belloc
ignores the conflict among the social classes and focuses instead on the
plight of the poor:

> Almighty God, whose justice like a sun
> Shall coruscate along the floors of Heaven,
> Raising what's low, perfecting what's undone,
> Breaking the proud and making odd things even,
> The poor of Jesus Christ along the street
> In your rain sodden, in your snows unshod,
> They have nor hearth, nor sword, nor human meat,
> Nor even the bread of men: Almighty God.                    (12)

The different perspectives on this situation are achieved through Belloc's careful use of the two genres. The satire is grimly cheerful, as befitting the confrontation between the rich man and the beggar. The sonnet, on the other hand, is almost a prayer to Christ to alleviate the suffering of the poor. The sonnet, the most popular genre of love poets, is perfectly appropriate for this different kind of love poem.

Social justice was one of Belloc's two major concerns at this time in his life. The other was Elodie, whom he married in 1896, soon after the publication of *Verses and Sonnets*. "The Harbour" dramatizes his frustration in waiting five years for her consent. Belloc uses a metaphor that was popular during the Renaissance in Europe:

> I was like one that keeps the deck by night
>     Bearing the tiller up against his breast;
> I was like one whose soul is centred quite
>     In holding course although so hardly prest,
> And veers with veering shock now left now right,
>     And strains his foothold still and still makes play
> Of bending beams until the sacred light
>     Shows him high lands and heralds up the day.          (9)

In "Love and Honour" he uses another favorite strategy of the Renaissance: the personification of abstract concepts. The impatient male is always Love, the reluctant female is Honour. In the traditional conflict Love tries unsuccessfully to conquer Honour, who retreats and thus conquers him by her virtue. After Belloc waits "a full five years' unrest," Honour appears to him one night:

> But when he saw her on the clear night shine
> Serene with more than mortal light upon her,
> The boy that careless was of things divine,
> Small Love, turned penitent to worship Honour.
>     So Love can conquer Honour: when that's past
>     Dead Honour risen outdoes Love at last.          (10)

Belloc loved Elodie, but he was also in love with English poetry.

Time, the enemy of all lovers, is the subject of many of the poems

in Belloc's first collection. In "Her Music" he expresses the fear that
the enchantment of his love will "stir strange hopes" of immortality,
"And make me dreamer more than dreams are wise" (10). The theme
of mutability is explored in the highlight of the volume, "Sonnets of
the Twelve Months," which contain some of Belloc's best descriptive
poetry. "January," for instance, contains this chilling portrait:

> Death, with his evil finger to his lip,
> Leers in at human windows, turning spy
> To learn the country where his rule shall lie
> When he assumes perpetual generalship.                    (3)

The brisk March wind is described in a line that combines perfectly
the sense and the sound: "Roaring he came above the white waves'
tips!" (4) The sonnets of the early summer months provide a gentle
interlude before the declining half of the year. In several of the sonnets
about the later months Belloc builds the poem around a famous
European battle scene. In "July," for instance, he describes the
Christian kings returning from the Crusades and states, "I wish to
God that I had been with them . . ." (6). In "August" Belloc's
historical imagination transports him to Charlemagne's great victory
at Roncesvalles. In "September" he becomes a participant in the
French Revolution: "But watching from that eastern casement, I /
Saw the Republic splendid in the sky, / And round her terrible head
the morning stars" (7). The best of the twelve sonnets is "December,"
which ends with this sestet:

> For now December, full of agéd care,
> Comes in upon the year and weakly grieves;
> Mumbling his lost desires and his despair;
> And with mad trembling hand still interweaves
> The dank sear flower-stalks tangled in his hair,
> While round about him whirl the rotten leaves.           (8)

This passage, reminiscent of *King Lear*, is an appropriate conclusion to
the sonnet sequence, for it unifies and transcends the individual battle
scenes in a final portrait of human suffering. Belloc's love of European
history, which was to become apparent in his numerous prose studies,
is here given its shape by the poet's sensibility.

Mankind's suffering and despair are not meaningless, however. Belloc focuses on the proud and defiant warriors, such as Charlemagne with his "bramble beard flaked red with foam / Of bivouac wine-cups . . . ," because they represent man's attempt to confront and conquer the forces of disorder and anarchy. Similarly, Belloc the poet enters into their world in his attempt to give meaning to their stories through his sonnets. "The sonnet," he wrote, "demands high verse more essentially than does any other looser form. . . .[T]he sonnet is the prime test of a poet."[22] In his first book he proudly announced his allegiance to the powers of poetry in its fight against the transience of man.

With his prose and then his parliamentary career occupying his time, Belloc did not publish his next volume of poetry until 1910. *Verses* includes many of the poems from *Verses and Sonnets*. Distinguishing the new verses from the old is not difficult, however, for the fourteen intervening years had changed Belloc dramatically. Whereas the first volume is marked by a youthful vitality and exuberance, *Verses* is permeated by a sense of spiritual fatigue and loss that characterized all of Belloc's work in the second half of his life. The death of his wife and then of his son Louis a few years later was to make this outlook permanent, but in 1910 Belloc was already beginning to characterize his life as a painful battle and to look backward to his youth as a carefree period of harmony with mankind and nature.

Yet the comic spirit is still alive in several poems. "Lines to a Don," for instance, is a comic diatribe against a "Remote and ineffectual Don / That dared attack my Chesterton" (153). It is full of cascading insults such as these:

> Don puffed and empty, Don dyspeptic;
> Don middle-class, Don sycophantic,
> Don dull, Don brutish, Don pedantic . . .          (153)

A comic self-portrait, "The Happy Journalist," describes Belloc's pleasures:

> I love to walk about at night
>   By nasty lanes and corners foul,
> All shielded from the unfriendly light

> And independent as the owl.                    (152)
> . . . . . . . . . . . . . . . .
> Policemen speak to me, but I,
>     Remembering my civic rights,
> Neglect them and do not reply.
>     I love to walk about at nights!          (153)

The comic verses, however, represent only a small part of the newer poetry. Belloc's alienation from society is portrayed most characteristically as violent combat. In "The Rebel," for example, he pictures himself as a soldier fighting against the forces of "lies and bribes." After describing how he would, like Paul Revere, "summon a countryside," and kill the evil men, he vows to:

> . . . batter their carven names,
> And slit the pictures in their frames,
> And burn for scent their cedar door,
> And melt the gold their women wore,
> And hack their horses at the knees . . .      (45)

In "The Prophet Lost in the Hills at Evening" this violent struggle is transferred to the battlefield of Belloc's soul as he envisions himself as God's warrior:

> I challenged and I kept the Faith,
>     The bleeding path alone I trod;
> It darkens. Stand about my wraith,
>     And harbour me, almighty God.              (46)

Belloc at this point in his life was a curious mixture of public ferocity and private anxiety. In public he was a courageous and selfless fighter, unafraid to elicit the wrath of the English people because of his unpopular pro-Boer stand, unafraid to speak out against the political corruption in his own party, and unafraid to attack the socialists, the atheists, and the Darwinians. Considering that he was always short of funds and that he could easily have earned far more money writing comic verse and less provocative histories, his decision to engage in these constant battles shows a remarkable strength of character. Poems such as "The Prophet," however, demonstrate the price he paid to maintain this public posture. Not only did he turn inward, he began to see himself as a divine messenger, a martyr who was being destroyed by the evil forces of the world.

The more successful poems in the 1910 collection are less self-consciously dramatic. "The South Country" pays homage to his native Sussex in simple and natural language:

> If I ever become a rich man,
>    Or if ever I grow to be old,
> I will build a house with deep thatch
>    To shelter me from the cold,
> And there shall the Sussex songs be sung
>    And the story of Sussex told.
>
> I will hold my house in the high wood
>    Within a walk of the sea,
> And the men that were boys when I was a boy
>    Shall sit and drink with me.                    (38)

Sussex became for Belloc not so much a county as a fortress. He was fully aware that this final scene is a fantasy, as are his self-portraits as a warrior or a religious martyr. The power of "The South Country" is his point that even though his dream is apparently humble, it is as unattainable as any attempt to turn back the clock.

The best poem in the collection, "Stanzas Written on Battersea Bridge During a South-Westerly Gale," dramatizes this thought rather than just stating it. Although Belloc never tired of criticizing Wordsworth, this poem shows that he learned the techniques of the meditative lyric from him. As his title suggests, the strategy of the poem is similar to Wordsworth's in "Lines Composed a Few Miles Above Tintern Abbey." Wordsworth begins his meditation by describing his impressions on revisiting the countryside that had meant so much to him when he was a boy. Belloc, on the other hand, pictures himself in London:

> The woods and downs have caught the mid-December,
>    The noisy woods and high sea-downs of home;
> The wind has found me and I do remember
>    The strong scent of the foam.                    (35)

After describing his desperate wish to return to Sussex and his youth, he realizes that:

> There is no Pilotry my soul relies on
>     Whereby to catch beneath my bended hand,
> Faint and beloved along the extreme horizon,
>     That unforgotten land.
>             . . . . . . . . . . . . . .
> Somewhere of English forelands grandly guarded
>     It stands, but not for exiles, marked and clean;
> Oh! not for us. A mist has risen and marred it:—
>     My youth lies in between.
>
> So in this snare that holds me and appals me,
>     Where honour hardly lives nor loves remain,
> The Sea compels me and my County calls me,
>     But stronger things restrain.
>                 . . .
> England, to me that never have malingered,
>     Nor spoken falsely, nor your flattery used,
> Nor even in my rightful garden lingered:—
>     What have you not refused?                    (35–36)

Unlike Wordsworth, whose realization of loss is tempered by a growth of understanding, Belloc sees no redemption in the passage of time. Like A. E. Housman, Belloc characterizes the journey from innocence to experience as a cruel joke. The last stanza is touched by an unreasonable self-pity, the indignation of a man who feels that his country has treated him unfairly—from the time of Oxford's refusal of the fellowship to his more recent struggles in the literary and political arenas. This treatment, Belloc is saying, is particularly unfair, considering the great energy he expended trying to do the right thing. Rather than remain in his "rightful garden"—the sheltered world of poetry—he confronted his enemies tirelessly.

But this self-pity is offset by the simple beauty of the last line. As W. H. Auden says in "In Memory of W. B. Yeats,"

> Time that is intolerant
>     Of the brave and innocent . . .
> Worships language and forgives
>     Everyone by whom it lives . . .[23]

Belloc never did understand the ways in which he made his life more difficult than it might have been. "Stanzas Written on Battersea Bridge" is a complete failure as a logical argument, but it is a beautiful and moving evocation of his confusion.

The 1910 volume received little critical notice. The *Times Literary Supplement*, however, called Belloc "specially successful with the music of a simple primitive rhythm."[24]

Belloc's analyses of the war occupied his mind during this period of personal loss; he wrote little poetry. His third book of verse, *Sonnets and Verse*, was not published until 1923, thirteen years after his second book, twenty-seven years after his first. By this time he had had a chance to contemplate his disappointments and his grief. Despite his increasing activity as a Catholic apologist, he never was able to integrate his personal experience and his faith. Almost all of the new poems included in the 1923 volume record Belloc's struggle to understand his tragedies; in none of them does he offer a Christian explanation. Like the classical poets whose work he studied and emulated, he remained essentially a pagan. And like the pagans who stoically accepted death, he finally came to an uneasy peace with his fate.

Not all of the poems, of course, concern death. "Tarantella" is a song about a subject Belloc knew well—"the fleas that tease in the High Pyrenees"—and "The Chanty of the 'Nona'" is a sea song commemorating a sail he took in 1914 along the western and southern coasts of England. For these songs, and for many others he wrote, he composed melodies that he loved to sing aloud. *Sonnets and Verse* also contains a number of stinging epigrams, such as "Epitaph on the Politician Himself":

> Here richly, with ridiculous display,
> The Politician's corpse was laid away.
> While all of his acquaintance sneered and slanged
> I wept: for I had longed to see him hanged. (114)

"On his Books" is a clever statement of a professional writer's aspirations:

> When I am dead, I hope it may be said:
> "His sins were scarlet, but his books were read." (112)

The mood of the volume, however, is most closely expressed by "The False Heart":

> I said to Heart, "How goes it?" Heart replied:
> "Right as a Ribstone Pippin!" But it lied.                                (112)

The bulk of *Sonnets and Verse* is love sonnets to Elodie. Several of them may in fact have been written before her death. The reader cannot tell because Belloc has stripped the poems down to an essential emotion—his love for her—which never changed in the sixty years following their first meeting. Any one of these sonnets demonstrates the timeless quality of his love:

> They that have taken wages of things done
> When sense abused has blocked the doors of sense,
> They that have lost their heritage of the sun,
> Their laughter and their holy innocence;
> They turn them now to this thing, now to t'other,
> For anchor hold against swift-eddying time,
> Some to that square of earth which was their mother,
> And some to noisy fame, and some to rhyme:
>
> But I to that far morning where you stood
> In fullness of the body, with your hands
> Reposing on your walls, before your lands,
> And all, together, making one great good:
>     Then did I cry "For this my birth was meant.
>     These are my use, and this my sacrament!"                    (15)

Belloc's definition of the sonnet form was very strict in one sense: he felt that the poet has to establish a clear break between the octave—the first eight lines—and the sestet—the other six. About the various rhyme schemes Belloc was silent, but he felt that the essence of the sonnet is the contrast between the unity of the octave and the response or elaboration of the sestet.

In this sonnet to Elodie the octave-sestet contrast embodies the meaning. The octave is the definition of how people attempt to deal with the passage of time. The first quatrain is Belloc's description of the ravages of time; the second quatrain is the description of how people react. Without identifying who these people are, he subtly distinguishes them from himself by using the distancing pronoun "they" in the first quatrain and the parallel grammatical structure in the second. Phrases such as "now to this thing, now to t'other" suggest the helplessness of these anonymous victims as they are buffeted uncontrollably by the seas of "swift-eddying time."

To the chaotic movement Belloc opposes his image of the stillness of Elodie. The contrast is introduced immediately by the transitional "But" and the first-person pronoun. His realization—the "cry" in the final couplet—is an exclamation of joy that contrasts with the "noisy fame" to which other people devote themselves. By creating this perfectly refined image of beauty, Belloc manages to cheat time. The point made by this poem is that his image may have occurred in 1900 or 1923. Man can freeze time in a memory, and an artist can convey that memory in a timeless work of art.

If several of Belloc's sonnets demonstrate the poet's ability to capture an image and thereby stop time, others confront the issue of Elodie's death directly. One attitude characteristic of some of these sonnets is the consolation that Elodie enjoyed and contributed to all of the valuable aspects of mortal life. This attitude is expressed, for instance, in the sestet of "When you to Acheron's ugly water come," in which Belloc describes the majesty and nobility with which Elodie died:

> Then go before them like a royal ghost
> And tread like Egypt or like Carthage crowned;
> Because in your Mortality the most
> Of all we may inherit has been found—
>   Children for memory: the Faith for pride;
>   Good land to leave: and young Love satisfied.          (17)

Unlike the "formless mourners" who stretch their hands longingly toward death, Elodie demonstrated in her death the grace she embodied in her life. Significantly, Belloc uses the pagan metaphor of crossing the river of death, despite his reference to the Catholic faith. His focus remains on the values of the living, not on the joys of the

Christian afterlife. This poem was probably written some years after her death, when he was finally able to write about it with a more peaceful stoicism.

If Belloc could ultimately accept Elodie's death in some of his poetry, he was less successful in dealing with it in his real life. He wrote, as late as 1922, one year before the publication of *Sonnets and Verse*, that "my cancer of loss gets worse and worse with every year and I grow fixed in the void of my wife and my son . . ."[25] Belloc never tried to forget his wife and son; on the contrary, he seems to have derived some solace from the rituals of grief. He wore only black from the day of Elodie's death, used funereal stationery, and traced the sign of the Cross upon her door before he went to bed every night at King's Land.[26]

Belloc's inability to let go of Elodie is dramatized in several of the poems in *Sonnets and Verse*. One sonnet in particular shows this response:

> We will not whisper, we have found the place
> Of silence and the endless halls of sleep:
> And that which breathes alone throughout the deep,
> The end and the beginning: and the face
> Between the level brows of whose blind eyes
> Lie plenary contentment, full surcease
> Of violence, and the passionless long peace
> Wherein we lose our human lullabies.
>
> Look up and tell the immeasurable height
> Between the vault of the world and your dear head;
> That's death, my little sister, and the night
> Which was our Mother beckons us to bed,
>     Where large oblivion in her house is laid
>     For us tired children, now our games are played.          (18)

Here Belloc pictures the death of his wife and himself as a peaceful sleep, a respite from the shocks of the world. Death will be safe, for he and Elodie are only children who are obeying their mother's request that they go to bed. In an epigram, "The Statue," he explores the same idea of his accompanying Elodie:

When we are dead, some Hunting-boy will pass
And find a stone half-hidden in tall grass
And grey with age: but having seen that stone
(Which was your image), ride more slowly on.         (113)

This beautiful and simple poem epitomizes *Sonnets and Verse*. The poet
and his beloved are now gone, but life continues as always on earth,
except that a passerby will be struck by her beauty as it is reflected by
her gravestone. These love poems that Belloc wrought out of his grief
were his memorial to Elodie. *Sonnets and Verse* thus represented for
him a catharsis. By defining himself as Elodie's companion, he was
able finally to stop the aching movement of time without his wife,
just as in the earlier love poems he was able to create a fixed image of
her.

The 1923 volume of poetry brought considerable critical reaction,
largely because Belloc had become by that time one of the best-known
English men of letters. An article in the *Saturday Review*, for example,
was titled "Mr. Belloc—Poet" and speculated that one of the reasons
he was not taken as seriously as a poet as he might have wished was
that he wrote so much prose. The anonymous reviewer suggested that
"he might, if he had confined himself to poetry, have been hailed as a
master . . ."[27] Along with several other commentators, the reviewer
argued that "it is in rare gleams of an essential and peculiar loveliness,
where the poet's strength and tenderness meet, that his bid for
immortality is made." Filson Young, writing in the *New York Times*,
also commented on the relative slimness of Belloc's poetic output:
"He seldom will condescend to be merely an artist, but in this book of
later poetry he returns, not without a shade of irony, to his old trade of
using language as an instrument to evoke beauty."[28] Belloc had
become a respected and admired poet of the classical style.

The final volume of poetry, also called *Sonnets and Verse* (1938), is
distinct from the 1923 volume in that it offers only a few brief lyrics to
the memory of Elodie. In all other respects, however, Belloc remained
unchanged. The generic classification system that the poet maintained emphasized this continuity. The "Epigrams" section of the
1923 volume, for instance, concludes with "Partly from the Greek."
The 1938 collection, without skipping a beat, simply continues with

the next epigram, "From the Same."

"The Fire," a melancholy description of how time has destroyed his hopes, is the best example of Belloc's later poetry. The self-assured pleasures of youth are described in the opening stanza, which gallops along carelessly in tetrameter lines.

> We rode together all in pride,
> They laughing in their riding gowns
> We young men laughing at their side,
> We charged at will across the downs.                    (78)

The assault by time, however, cannot be resisted: "The golden faces charged with sense / Have broken to accept the years" (78). The speaker, now alone and perplexed, demonstrates Belloc's ability to change the tone radically while maintaining the tetrameter lines:

> Were they not here, the girls and boys?
> I hear them. They are at my call.
> The stairs are full of ghostly noise,
> But there is no one in the hall.                        (78)

Also characteristic of Belloc are the biting epigrams. One victim is a pacifist: "Pale Ebenezer thought it wrong to fight, / But Roaring Bill (who killed him) thought it right" (118). Another victim, a Puritan, Belloc would classify a religious eccentric: "He served his God so faithfully and well / That now he sees him face to face, in hell" (118). And, as always, Belloc loved to define the political animal, as in "On Two Ministers of State":

> Lump says that Caliban's of gutter breed,
> And Caliban says Lump's a fool indeed,
> And Caliban and Lump and I are all agreed.              (118)

Belloc's poetic masterpiece, "Heroic Poem in Praise of Wine," is also included in the 1938 *Sonnets and Verse.* Both poetically and philosophically, it is his most mature composition. The term "heroic poem" in the title refers to the poetic form: rhymed iambic pentameter couplets, sometimes called heroic couplets or heroic verse. By choosing this demanding poetic form for a work of over two hundred lines, he was distinguishing himself from the world of modern poetry and allying himself with the classical Greek and Roman writers and, in England, with Dryden and Pope.

Belloc chose the heroic couplet because it complemented the world and the spirit he wanted to celebrate:

> To exalt, enthrone, establish and defend,
> To welcome home mankind's mysterious friend:
> Wine, true begetter of all arts that be;
> Wine, privilege of the completely free;
> Wine the recorder; wine the sagely strong;
> Wine, bright avenger of sly-dealing wrong,
> Awake, Ausonian Muse, and sing the vineyard song! (80)

This classical invocation leads into a description of Bacchus, driving his chariot pulled by a team of panthers, swooping down over Europe and creating, everywhere, "The Vines, the conquering Vines!" (1. 35)

After this definition of the creation of the vineyards, Belloc begins his greatest passage of high comic verse:

> But what are these that from the outer murk
> Of dense mephitic vapours creeping lurk
> To breathe foul airs from that corrupted well
> Which oozes slime along the floor of Hell?
> These are the stricken palsied brood of sin
> In whose vile veins, poor, poisonous and thin,
> Decoctions of embittered hatreds crawl:
> These are the Water-Drinkers, cursed all!
> On what gin-sodden Hags, what flaccid sires
> Bred these White Slugs from what exhaust desires? (82)

The conflict between the misguided water-drinkers and the godly wine-drinkers is not resolved; despite his comic treatment, Belloc is portraying nothing less than the struggle of Catholics "in these last unhappy days / When beauty sickens and a muddied robe / Of baseness fouls the universal globe" (84).

The final movement of the poem begins on an elegiac note:

> When from the waste of such long labour done
> I too must leave the grape-ennobling sun
> And like the vineyard worker take my way
> Down the long shadows of declining day,
> Bend on the sombre plain my clouded sight
> And leave the mountain to the advancing night,
> Come to the term of all that was mine own
> With nothingness before me, and alone;
> Then to what hope of answer shall I turn?                    (86)

Raising his chalice of sacramental wine to the God he cannot see, he prepares to reenter "my Father's Kingdom." "Heroic Poem in Praise of Wine" combines a sustained technical virtuosity with Belloc's most sophisticated vision: a subtle mingling of the pagan earth and the Christian sky. He worked on the poem for some twenty years.[29] More important, however, he lived most of his life before he could understand and articulate—just this once—the essential unity of comedy and tragedy on earth.

The critical essay that most insightfully defines how the 1938 volume illuminated Belloc appeared in *The Catholic World*: " . . . the volume contains more than one indication that his faith, robust and virile as it is, has been wrested from the teeth of doubt."[30] The other journals concentrated on Belloc's pursuit of the classical poetic virtues of craftsmanship, control, precision, and clarity of expression. The *Times Literary Supplement* contrasted Belloc with the "new severe young men" who sacrificed form for intellectual content.[31] Critic George Sampson wrote, in 1941, that:

Belloc's serious poems, slight in quantity, are exquisite in quality. His sonnets are the finest modern examples of that much tried form. His songs can laugh and laud and deride with the ribald vigour of the past and the effective point of the present. No one in recent times has touched sacred themes with such appealing delicacy. The poems of Belloc show triumphantly how a modern writer can follow an old tradition and remain master of himself.[32]

Belloc was characteristically—and extravagantly—humble about his poetry. He once wrote that "I am one who by nature writes commonplace verse, which I then slowly tinker at and turn into less commonplace."[33] He did not believe this for an instant, of course, but just as he refused to call his verse "poetry"—a term he considered too exalted for his efforts—he would not allow himself a public display of pride. But when the critics praised the poems he sculpted and polished, Belloc must have smiled inwardly.

## Chapter Three
# The Histories

Although Hilaire Belloc worked in every major genre but drama, he thought of himself as primarily a historian. His academic training at Oxford was in history, and the largest single category of his voluminous output was historical studies. More intensely than any other contemporary historian, Belloc examined the relationship between religion and politics in European history since the Middle Ages. The phenomenon that he studied in most of his work was the process by which Catholic, monarchist Europe became Protestant and republican.

## Belloc's Concept of History

Like all serious historians, Belloc felt that a knowledge of the past was not merely a social grace, but an indispensable part of responsible citizenship. Only by studying history, he often said, could one hope to understand the evolution of modern civilization and to participate constructively in society.

In Belloc's estimation, the historian has the most difficult job of any writer since it is necessary for him to manage several tasks simultaneously.

[The historian] must keep his imagination active; his style must be not only lucid, but also must arrest the reader; he must exercise perpetually a power of selection which plays over innumerable details; he must, in the midst of such occupations, preserve unity of design, as much as must the novelist or the playwright; and yet with all this there is not a verb, an adjective or a substantive which, if it does not repose upon established evidence, will not mar the particular type of work on which he is engaged.[1]

Belloc believed that, in the words of the French historian Michelet, history should be "a resurrection of the flesh." Accordingly, extraordinary vividness and immediacy characterize Belloc's historical writing. Although he devoted ample space in his studies to what he called the "circumstance"—the philosophical, political, religious, and economic conditions of the period—his specialty was the evocation of the human experience. He usually wrote from the perspective of the eyewitness, not the aloof and objective scholar. Unlike most historians, Belloc described the weather, the time of day, the clothing and physical appearance of the major participants, and even the sounds in the air.

Belloc's research for a historical study included his studying not only the standard documents and histories; he also visited the important sites, especially the battlefields. He stood where Napoleon stood in Moscow, and he paced off the territory near Valmy where the Prussian forces failed to pierce the French revolutionary defenses. He sat in the room from which Robespierre saw Danton being led off to the guillotine. He studied obscure local documents for the smallest details that would help him recreate a particular moment from the past.

Despite this exhaustive research, he incurred the scathing criticism of the historical establishment for a very simple reason: he refused to include the traditional scholarly apparatus—the footnotes and bibliography—in his books. His defense was that he was writing not for the scholar, but for the general reader, who is uninterested in "the misfortunes of official academic history."[2] Interrupting the text for footnotes, Belloc wrote, would destroy the continuity of his narrative and prove a distraction. In a comic essay entitled "On Footnotes" he contrasts his own method with that of the scholars:

I notice that when anything is published without such footnotes, the professional critic—himself a footnoter of the deepest dye—accuses the author of romancing. If you put in details of the weather, of dress and all the rest of it, minutely gathered from any amount of reading, but refuse to spoil a vivid narrative with the snobbery and charlatanism of these perpetual references, the opponent takes it for granted that you have not kept your notes and cannot answer him; and indeed, as a rule, you have not kept your notes and you cannot answer him.[3]

Belloc believed that most footnotes are simply copied directly from previously published sources, that scholars compound the errors and faulty judgments of their predecessors rather than check the original documents themselves. For this reason, several of Belloc's studies include as appendices transcripts of original documents, introduced by his comments. Only on a few occasions does he refer to another historian.

A personal motive probably contributed to Belloc's avoidance of the traditional techniques. When he was denied the history fellowship at Oxford, he became deeply embittered. The rejection became a symbol that the historical establishment deemed him unworthy. For half a century after his humiliation he waged a ceaseless war against his enemies. If they used the scholarly apparatus, he would not. Rather than relegate his documentation to endnotes and appendices, where it would not interrupt his narrative—a technique he recognized as rational but did not use after his first few histories—he simply refused to include the documentation at all. The prefaces of most of his historical studies begin with almost identical defenses of his style: even though he has not provided traditional documentation for his assertions, he trusts that his arguments are justified sufficiently within the narrative itself.

## Belloc's Historical Thesis

Belloc's quarrel with the historical establishment extended beyond the question of scholarly technique. Like all historians, he believed that history is not a collection of facts, but a coherent explanation of complex events. In the Preface to *Robespierre* (1901), his second historical study, for example, he defines the writing of history as an organic, creative act: "It is like the growing of slow timber upon a sheltered hill; you seem to have established an enduring thing . . . then, when reality is reached, it is easy to be sure; and . . . so much doubt and contradiction are resolved into a united history."[4] Yet the thesis he evolved, his idea of historical "reality," always appeared radical to the scholarly community. Following his disillusioning experience in Parliament, he wrote a series of studies on English history, concentrating on the monarchs of the seventeenth century. Arguing that the Reformation was the central disaster of Western civilization because it not only separated mankind from the true religion but also created the "Money Powers" who oppressed the average citizen, Belloc advocated a return to a system of government led by a strong monarch who would protect the rights of the weak. This thesis set him in clear opposition to what he called "the official Whig historians." According to Belloc, Whig scholars such as Thomas Babington Macaulay, G. M. Trevelyan, and Albert Frederick Pollard argued "that the rich should govern, and that the most horrible of all political evils is a popular monarchy strong enough to control the powerful and protect the oppressed. It is the theory of the mid-nineteenth century tea-table in the large country house."[5] In his more charitable mood Belloc asserted that the established historians had a lesser regard for truth than he; more often, he simply called them liars.[6]

Belloc was an intensely proud man, and rather than tone down his overstatement or accommodate the conventions of his chosen profession—when it would have been so easy to do—he preferred to defy and provoke his detractors by writing the kind of compelling and vital narratives they could not write. That would be his revenge.

Belloc made a conscious decision. For the general reader, he is certainly one of the most accessible and interesting commentators on European and English history. As a serious academic historian, he has been discredited. Because of his pro-Catholic and pro-monarchist perspective and his disregard for the standard scholarly techniques, the critical assessment of his historical studies is almost unanimous. Leonard Woolf's response to *James the Second* in the *Nation and Athenaeum* is representative: "Mr. Belloc makes this myth into a rattling good story, which I certainly enjoyed reading."[7]

## The Studies of the French Revolution

In the first decade and a half of his professional writing career Belloc produced *Danton, Robespierre, Marie Antoinette, The French Revolution*, and *High Lights of the French Revolution*. Taken together, these five books constitute his best and most representative work in history. In *Danton* Belloc approached his most congenial subject; Danton was a personal hero of a heroic movement. *Robespierre* was a far more difficult task, for although Belloc could understand his role in the revolution, he could never understand the man himself. *Marie*

*Antoinette* posed the most problems for Belloc because he had little sympathy for what she represented. Yet in writing the book he was forced to recognize that the unimaginative and frivolous queen, who had little practical effect on the revolution, achieved a tragic stature in death that she lacked throughout her life. *The French Revolution* is probably Belloc's best account of a historical phenomenon: it is balanced, objective, and comprehensive. *High Lights of the French Revolution* shows Belloc's skill as a miniaturist, recreating the human drama of selected episodes of the revolution. In creating these murals, portraits, and cameos of the French Revolution, the young Hilaire Belloc exhibited all of his skills as a historian.

While Belloc was establishing his reputation as a writer of comic and satiric verse in the last years of the nineteenth century, he was at work on his first historical study, *Danton* (1899), which for many readers remains the greatest of his many biographies. Writing with an energy and enthusiasm that he was never to recapture, Belloc immersed himself in his analysis of the French Revolution's first great architect.

The French Revolution had always fascinated Belloc, for he saw it as a watershed moment in Western civilization:

. . . it rebuilt from the foundations. How many unquestioned dogmas were suddenly brought out into broad daylight! All our modern indecision, our confused philosophies, our innumerable doubts, spring from that stirring of the depths. Is property a right? . . . Is marriage sacred? Have we duties to the State, to the family? . . . Occasionally a man suddenly rises and asks, "Is there a God?" (9)

And still in his twenties, Belloc saw the French Revolution as not only crucial, but basically good; it was a "reversion to the normal—a sudden and violent return to those conditions which are the necessary bases of health in any political community" (1).

If the Revolution was a noble but tragic experiment in republicanism, Danton was its tragic hero. As Belloc explains in the Preface to the book,

. . . in the saving of France, when the men of action were needed . . . he leaps to the front. . . . [T]he whole nation and its story becomes filled with his name. . . . Danton, his spirit, his energy, his practical grasp of things as they were, formed the strength of France. . . . All that was useful in the Terror was his work; and if we trace . . . the actions that swept the field and left it ready for rapid organization and defence . . . we nearly always find his masterful and sure guidance. (xi)

The Danton that emerges from the book suggests another reason for Belloc's attraction. In his physical appearance, personality, and turn of mind, Danton bears a striking resemblance to Belloc:

He was tall and stout, with the forward bearing of the orator, full of gesture and animation. He carried a round French head upon the thick neck of energy. (53)

. . .

In his politics he desired above all actual, practical, and apparent reforms; changes for the better expressed in material results. . . . It was a part of something in his character . . . (55)

What is most interesting, Belloc defines in Danton the self-assured dogmatism that he himself was to be accused of only a few years later:

He seems to have lacked almost entirely the metaphysic. . . . Reform should be practical: in part it would require discussion, not too much of it. . . . [H]is was . . . that confused instinct which is, after all, nearest to the truth. Patriotism, good fellowship, freedom for his activities, the satisfaction of the thirst for knowledge—all these he desired for himself and for the State. (67—68)

The book chronicles the process by which Danton created the new French republic, organized its defense against the armies of a united monarchist Europe, and eventually was guillotined by the more radical republican forces led by Robespierre. The highlight of *Danton* for the general reader is the closing chapter, in which Belloc employs all of his descriptive skills in evoking his hero's last hour, as he and his fellow victims are being led to their death. Rather than restricting his scope to the beheading itself, Belloc includes the peripheral elements that give the event its dramatic significance: "the air was warm and pleasant, the leaves and the buds were out on the few trees, the sky was unclouded. All that fatal spring was summerlike, and this day was the calmest and most beautiful that it had known. The light, already tinged with evening, came flooding the houses of the north bank till their glass shone in the eyes" (273—74). Amidst the jostling crowds and the lengthening shadows, Danton on the scaffold awaiting his death sings a song predicting the death of Robespierre and then laughs heartily. Belloc's attitude toward Danton is clear: "I will end this book by that last duty of mourning, as we who hold to immortality yet break our hearts for the dead" (318).

The subject of his next historical biography, Robespierre, was a logical choice, for the leader of the bloody Reign of Terror was the most important and powerful figure in revolutionary France between Danton and Napoleon. In another sense, however, Robespierre was not the logical choice for Belloc's next major work, for, unlike Danton, he lacked the sweeping and magnetic personality that the historian could transform into an exciting narrative. As Belloc writes in the Preface to *Robespierre* (1901), reconstructing the revolutionary's life has been so difficult "I could almost wish that instead of wandering in such a desert it had been my task to follow St. Just and the wars, and to revive the memories of forgotten valour" (xiii).

Valor has no part in Belloc's portrait of Robespierre, a man who seemed an unlikely revolutionary. With his conservative and understated clothing and his powdered wig, he appeared the perfect representative of the old regime. And his oratory—full of ornate classical allusions and modulated rhythms—was antithetical to that of the fiery Danton. Whereas Danton was the spokesman for the practical expedient, Robespierre cared only for the pure rationalism of Rousseau's *Social Contract*, the seminal pamphlet of democracy and republicanism. Robespierre's single-minded adherence to his understanding of Rousseau was, in Belloc's mind, what enabled him to permit the revolution to pursue its dictatorial course during the Reign of Terror.

Robespierre allowed the idea to take precedence over humanity because he himself was separate from humanity. He was "a man all conviction and emptiness, too passionless to change, too iterant to be an artist, too sincere and tenacious to enliven folly with dramatic art or to save it by flashes of its relation to wisdom. When so many loved and hated men or visions, till their great souls turned them into soldiers, he knew nothing but his truth and was untroubled" (38). Over and over, Belloc defines Robespierre as "mechanical, uncreative" (109), a "nonentity" (103). One passage in the book is particularly interesting as it reveals Belloc's difficulties in restricting himself to Robespierre the man:

Hitherto I have followed through this chapter the fortunes and opinions of a man whom Nature had not intended to be great, and to whom the accident of the Revolution has as yet given nothing but a steadfast, brilliant, and fictitious popularity. I have shut out the general picture by standing within his closed mind. . . . But here . . . the insignificance of such a theme appals me, and I see that not even the truth about this one individual can be made plain unless some glimpse of that portentous background is admitted to the scene. (175)

Writing about Robespierre and thus becoming caught up in the revolution "is like sitting up in a darkened room throughout the night upon some exact calculation, and at last to look up by chance and see through the shutters that it is dawn. Then one abandons for a moment the ceaseless labour of mechanical details, and throws open the windows to the air and the day" (175).

Robespierre's dry precision was one reason that Belloc could not forge an imaginative link with him, but his effect on the course of the revolution was the more important factor. In the turbulent year of 1793 he allowed the revolution to pursue its violent course so that he could maintain control over the radical revolutionaries. Belloc argues that had Robespierre lent his considerable prestige and power to the cause of the moderates, he might have prevented some of the excesses of the Reign of Terror, the bloodletting that cost twenty thousand lives. For Belloc, Robespierre thus betrayed not only himself and the spirit of Danton, but the spirit of the revolution.

Like Danton, Robespierre was put to death by his fellow revolutionaries. His death was the more gruesome, for he had received what probably would have been a fatal gunshot wound in the face shortly before his execution. "He gave, as they loosened his bandage, a loud cry of pain. The axe fell, and powder shook from his hair" (367).

In spite of his difficulties with Robespierre, Belloc's final assessment is qualified admiration: "I fear I have done him a wrong. Such men may be greater within than their phrases or their vain acts display them. I know that he passed through a furnace of which our paltry time can reimagine nothing, and I know that throughout this trial he affirmed—with monotonous inefficiency, but still affirmed—the fundamental truths" (366–67).

His study of Robespierre complete, Belloc wanted to turn to St. Just, another warrior who upheld "the fundamental truths." But Methuen, the publishing house to which Belloc was financially indebted, insisted that he choose for his next subject a much more popular figure with the reading public, Marie Antoinette.[8] The resulting book took Belloc five long and painful years. In a letter to a friend written in 1909 (when *Marie Antoinette* was published), he admitted that he had an aversion to the thought of writing about her, and that it took him three years to understand her character. "And indeed my appreciation of the anti-revolutionary position has become very strong in the last two years."[9]

Belloc's comment would suggest that *Marie Antoinette* is an unsympathetic and unenthusiastic piece of hack work; on the contrary, it is one of his best biographies. For one thing, it forced Belloc to reexamine his point of view about the period and to confront a character who clearly was not central to the course of the revolution. Whereas in his studies of Danton and Robespierre Belloc knew essentially his thesis before he began the arduous research, in studying Marie Antoinette he had to create his thesis out of his research. In addition, the study forced him to examine the human tragedies of the revolution with a concentration and compassion that had been lacking in the two earlier studies. The executions of Danton and Robespierre were simply the final chapters in the lives of two pivotal characters of the revolution. The trial and execution of Marie Antoinette were the *only* important events, and even they were irrelevant to the revolution: Louis XVI had already been executed.

Belloc was fully aware that the plan for *Marie Antoinette* had to be different from that of his other biographies. As he writes in an Introductory Note, "The eighteenth century, which had lost the appetite for tragedy and almost the comprehension of it, was granted, before it closed, the most perfect subject of tragedy which history affords. . . . In person she was not considerable, in temperament not distinguished; but her fate was enormous" (vii). In writing the tragedy of Marie Antoinette, Belloc for the first time in his career was able to identify fully with his subject, to repress his own viewpoint and see the world from her perspective. He did not disappear completely, of course—the book is marred by some unnecessary Catholic propaganda—but in crucial passages he was able to evoke the personality of Marie Antoinette by an act of imaginative identification.

The description of Marie Antoinette's learning of the fall of the Bastille, for example, captures all of her fear and self-confidence: "the tumult was a mere civilian tumult: the thousands roaring in Paris had no arms—and then what about organisation? How can a mob organise? Tuesday came, the 14th of July, a memorable day, and in the forenoon news or rumours reached Versailles that a stock of arms had been sacked" (211). Perhaps the greatest passage of dramatic identification is Belloc's description of the imprisoned queen waiting for the final visit of the king as he is led off to the guillotine:

> For a moment there were voices in the courtyard, the tramp of many men upon the damp gravel, the creaking of the door, more distant steps in the gardens, and the wheels of the coach far away at the outer porch. Then the confused noise of a following crowd dwindling westward till nothing remained but a complete silence in those populous streets, now deserted upon so great a public occasion. . . . [After another hour] the Queen heard through the shuttered window the curious and dreadful sound of a crowd that roars far off, and she knew that the thing had been done. (346−47)

The last chapter of *Marie Antoinette*, "Wattignies," alternates descriptions of that critical battle with a narrative of the queen's excruciating trial. In writing the book, Belloc learned to recognize the heroic stoicism that can exist in persons who have nothing to do with the fundamental truths.

After completing his study of Marie Antoinette, Belloc accepted the invitation of a friend, H. A. L. Fisher, to write a history of the French Revolution for the Home University Library.[10] *The French Revolution* (1911) was an easy task for Belloc. His research for the three early biographies enabled him to dictate this text virtually without stopping to check a reference.[11] Working quickly, he was able to block out a clear and rational plan that prevented the biases and distortions that marred many of his other histories. Thus, he treated first the political theory of the revolution, concentrating on the influence of Rousseau's *Social Contract*. Next, he balanced his discussion of the intellectual climate with a series of nine brief character sketches, including, among others, the royal couple, Lafayette, Danton, and Robespierre. Three other major sections followed: the phases of the revolution, the military history, and the role of the Catholic Church.

The study is a brisk and absorbing overview of a very complicated phenomenon, but Belloc's particular skills are evident in a number of lively descriptions. The sketch of the wealthy Lafayette, for instance, concludes with this comment: "One anecdote out of many will help to fix his nature in the mind of the reader. Mirabeau, casting about as usual for aid in his indebtedness sent urgently to him as a fellow noble, a fellow politician and a fellow supporter of the Crown, begging a loan of £2000: La Fayette accorded him £1,000"(66–67). Another example of Belloc's skill is his explanation of the European forces' inability to break through the French line at the battle of Valmy. Using his peculiar combination of historical imagination and on-site research, he speculates that the wet autumn weather made the clay soil impassable for the guns and wagons of the attacking forces. This small accident of fate gave the ill-equipped and disheartened French troops the self-confidence they needed to turn back the more powerful European armies.

*The French Revolution* was Belloc's academic study of the period. He returned to the revolution six years later with *High Lights of the French Revolution* (1916),[12] a collection of six dramatic vignettes including the storming of the Bastille, the royal couple's unsuccessful escape attempt to Varennes, and the execution of the king. In the earlier book Belloc attempted to portray objectively and dispassionately the causes and the events of the revolution, but in *High Lights* he isolates several episodes that epitomized the confusion, excitement, and terror of the period. The difference between the two styles is apparent in the description of the battle at Valmy.

In *The French Revolution* Belloc had described the aborted Prussian offensive in this way:

That charge was never carried home; whether, as some believe, because it was discovered, after it was ordered, to be impossible in the face of the accuracy and intensity of the French fire, or whether, as is more probably the case, because the drenched soil compelled the commanders to abandon the movement after it had begun—whatever the cause may have been, the Prussian force, though admirably disciplined and led, and though advancing in the most exact order, failed to carry out its original purpose. (166)

In *High Lights* the same action is described thus:

This was the opportunity for the charge, and Brunswick sent forward one . . . [of] . . . the companies of the famous Prussian line. They began their descent into the shallow valley—a slow descent, their boots clogged by pounds of the field mud, a perilous advance, with their own guns firing over their heads across the valley, but an advance which, when it should be complete, the half-mile crossed, and the opposing slope taken at the charge, would descend to the business of the invasion, and would end the resistance of the Revolutionary armies. Against them as they went forward was now directed some part of the French artillery fire, such part as could be spared from the Prussian guns above. (187)

The first description begins with a statement of the outcome and then offers the various explanations for the failure of the assault. The second description is written from the perspective of the Prussian soldier as he trudges across the muddy field with the artillery fire screaming above his head. Belloc never forgot that, in addition to being the decisive event in the formulation of the modern world, the French Revolution was a vast spectacle of human courage and suffering.

Belloc's studies of the French Revolution were greeted by the critical extremes that were to persist throughout his career. *Danton* and *The French Revolution* received high praise, but the review of *Marie Antoinette* published in the *Nation* typifies the response to the other works: "His book is about as untrustworthy a performance as ever came from the pen of a master of rhetoric—which is saying a good deal. And yet Mr. Belloc is a most brilliant writer, and capable of thought; and one enjoys his bad book—as a romance."[13] From his first historical study to his last, Belloc was acknowledged to be a brilliant

writer. But the warning flags—about his emphasis and accuracy—
were raised.

## A History of England

Belloc's most ambitious historical project was his four-volume *A History of England* (1925, 1927, 1928, 1931), which begins with the earliest recorded history and concludes with the death in 1612 of Robert Cecil, the leading statesman of Elizabethan England. Belloc's original plan encompassed English history up to 1900; at one point, he envisioned a seven-volume study. Fatigue was one factor that led him to abandon the tremendous project. More important, however, was the fact that in covering the Reformation he considered the essential task complete. For, according to Belloc, the creation of republican England and the civil war of the seventeenth century were inevitable outgrowths of the rise and official sanctioning of Protestantism in Henry VIII's reign. The four volumes in effect constitute a history of Catholic England.

The indefinite article "a" in the title of Belloc's history suggests that it was to be radically different in perspective from the existing histories. In all of the volumes he attacked relentlessly the "official Whig historians," those who saw the origins of medieval England in the Germanic invasions of the Dark Ages, and who saw in the overthrow of Catholicism and monarchy the fortunate birth of modern capitalist, republican England.

As always, Belloc took the offensive in the battle and declared his intentions openly. The Preface to the first volume, for instance, states: "The author has attempted . . . to combine considerable detail of narrative and date with the presence of general thesis; as, that religion is the determining force of society, that the inhabitants of the island were never greatly changed in stock by any invasion; that its institutions derive not from any imaginary barbaric German ancestry, but from known and recorded Roman civilization" (v-vi). The religion of pagan England was "ignorant of the One True God, and therefore cruel and despairing" (7). Belloc maintained this deliberately provocative emphasis on religion throughout the four volumes. In the fourth, for example, he asserts that the "ultimate dependence of all the main social phenomena upon religion" gives the sixteenth and seventeenth centuries their meaning and interest, despite "the tedious accompaniment of dates and political details"(7).

In fact, much of *A History* is tedious for the general reader. When Belloc is not describing the personalities and events of Catholic history, his narrative sometimes becomes a dry recitation of minor details. In the earlier volumes especially, the paucity of historical record prevents him from creating the vivid and evocative character sketches and imaginative re-creations of events that are his specialty. In the first volume, for instance, he feels obliged to mention three local governors ruling after A.D. 122—Falco, Platorius Nepos, and Sextus Severus—even though he admits that little is known of them except their names (82).

When he had raw material, however, and when he was interested in the subject, Belloc wrote absorbing history. Describing the conflict between Henry II and Thomas à Becket, he objectively defines the king's argument, then the Church's. Finally, he sums up the conflict: "Either there was to be an independent Church ruling all the lives of Christian men in what all agreed to be the most important things; or there was to be a lay State wherein the Church would become at long last a mere sect—an opinion" (2:203). And even though Belloc announces his preference unequivocally, the analysis remains informative and compelling.

The critical response to *A History of England* was characteristic: every commentator agreed that Belloc had a fine narrative gift, and almost every one agreed that his emphasis on the religious struggle was disproportionate. The fact that Belloc followed his usual practice of omitting the normal scholarly apparatus made him an easy target for his detractors. In the first volume he defended himself by stating that continual reference would be "impossible" (vi); in the second volume, he argued that he was "giving the reader the main truths of history, without the confusion of manifold reference . . ." (xi); in the third volume, he asked his readers to judge whether he was persuasive.

Belloc knew as early as 1916, when he began *A History*, that he was going to ignore the scholarly conventions. He wrote to a friend, declaring that his style would be "readable stuff fairly persuasive," rather than "bald statement, take it or leave it."[14] Unfortunately,

Belloc never believed that one could write "readable stuff very persuasive."

## The Studies of Monarchy

In the last fifteen years of his active writing career—from about 1925 to 1940—Belloc focused his historical work on the great monarchs of France and England. In the years since his first analyses of the French Revolution his belief in the ideals of liberty, equality, and fraternity remained ardent, but his thoughts on how to achieve those ideals changed radically. While he admitted that republican England had grown tremendously in population, wealth, and political liberty, he felt that the destruction of a powerful monarchy by Parliament had led to the economic enslavement of the average citizen. The corruption and inefficiency of Parliament that he had witnessed convinced him that a return to monarchy—by which he meant any form of centralized authority—was necessary in order to protect the weak wage-earner from "the Money Power."

Belloc's studies concentrated on the reigns of Louis XIII and Louis XIV in France, and on the English monarchs from Henry VIII in the early sixteenth century to James II in the late seventeenth. The following discussion examines several of these books to show the evolution of Belloc's conception of the study of monarchy.

When Belloc was asked by an American publisher to write a biography of Richelieu, he agreed on the condition that the firm would publish first his study of James II of England. When the publisher accepted the terms, Belloc traveled to El Kantara, on the edge of the African desert, and in eight days wrote *James the Second* (1928). [15]

The career of James II, who ruled England from 1685–1688, interested Belloc because it represented the fatal intertwining of character and circumstance. James was a singularly ineffective king because he was unable to understand human motivation. He believed that everyone was as honest and guileless as he:

. . . every betrayal and falsehood bewildered him. Each came with a new shock. He learnt from none. He could not believe that his officers would desert him. He could not believe that his daughters would abandon him, usurp his throne. . . . His enemies—at least those of posterity—find something ridiculous in such naiveté. He should have known better. The trusting man is a fool. But something deeper appears in all this than matter for scorn. A dupe may be noble. (28)

The nobility that attracted Belloc to James II was his willingness to declare openly his Catholicism and so jeopardize his rule. Parliament, vehemently Protestant, interpreted James's open avowal as a threat to its religion and thus set in motion the Glorious Revolution of 1688, which assured Protestant continuity by installing as rulers William and his wife Mary, James's Protestant daughter. James precipitated his own downfall by advocating religious toleration. Charles II, James's older brother and the previous king, had also personally favored religious toleration, but had bowed to parliamentary pressure and withdrawn his support. James, however, was a different man; he did not understand how allowing equal religious rights would constitute a threat to the overwhelmingly Protestant country.

James thus resembled Belloc, who always attributed his great professional setback—the denial of the Oxford fellowship—to his outspoken Catholicism. His entire career—at this point entering its last phase—had been determined by his stubborn refusal to make peace with his enemies, the established historians. Even though they repeatedly acknowledged his great talent, he refused to try to understand them. In choosing to begin his study of monarchy with the "noble dupe" whose willful blindness accelerated the destruction of the English monarchy, Belloc was unconsciously repeating the tendency that had become apparent three decades earlier with *Danton*. In his youth he had hoped to be Danton; entering late middle age, he had become James II.

After studies of the principal advisors of Louis XIII and Henry VIII, Belloc turned to the king who reaped the bitter fruits of Henry's split from Rome. In calling his book *Charles the First* (1933), Belloc suggested that he was interested in Charles primarily—if not exclusively—because of the effect he had on the institution of monarchy. This point is made clear on the first page of the book. "In England a rebellion three hundred years ago deposed and killed the King. Thenceforward the wealthier classes who had raised that rebellion gradually ousted the Crown and took over its power. How and why did English kingship so fail in the person of its last possessor, Charles Stuart? That is the problem approached in this book" (13).

The tone is established by Belloc's central thesis: that any historical phenomenon such as the execution of Charles is made up of two elements—"circumstance" and "the character of the man"—and that the circumstance in this case, the growth of parliamentary power, made the killing of the king likely, and even probable, but certainly not inevitable. The personality of Charles "rendered the evil more certain [and] gave it the shape it took" (16).

Belloc condemned Charles's weakness in crucial circumstances, such as his bowing to Parliament's display of power when it contrived charges against Strafford, one of his advisors. In a skillful passage such as the following Belloc exhibits his great ability to combine a striking image of an event and a chilling statement of its implications: "When a man of sensitive conscience and high honour is torn between various imperative duties, he will bear remorse till death for whatever course he has taken; for thus abandoning Strafford and securing a brief precarious peace among his people Charles bled inward tears of blood to the day of his own death by the same violence" (259). Charles's fate was sealed for him precisely because he was a man of sensitive conscience and high honor. Like his son James II, he lacked completely the gifts of intrigue and duplicity—"all those talents which make for the greatness of a statesman" (309). Belloc did express a grudging admiration for Charles's valiant battle against the physical limitations that almost took his life as a child. Yet his final reaction to Charles's life was sadness and disappointment: Charles made himself the best man he could be, but he could not become a king powerful enough to withstand the enormous conflicts in seventeenth-century England. With Charles died the heritage of effective monarchy in England.

Charles's chief antagonist is the subject of Belloc's next historical study, *Cromwell* (1934). He looked forward to writing the book not only because it would complement his previous study, but also because Cromwell was "a man on whom the official English history has lied more freely than on anybody else."[16] Belloc's starting point for the study was "the huge double myth" of Oliver Cromwell. The first myth, which was born with the restoration of Charles II in 1660, is that Cromwell was a traitor, a dictator, and a coward. The second myth, which grew in the nineteenth century, argues that he was a national hero, the "Chief Man of a Superior Race" (13). The truth, according to Belloc, is that Cromwell was a brilliant military tactician who was unable to lead the state he created:

The man was compelled, in sheer self-preservation, to get another man out of the way. He did save himself with singular tenacity and yet more remarkable skill; he carried out his plan thoroughly concealing intention, keeping in the background, employing agents privately, pleading doubtfully for the victim in public. He succeeded and Charles Stuart was brought to the scaffold. The plot so achieved is well worth admiring . . . (16)

In elaborating this argument, Belloc begins by tracing Cromwell's ancestry back a century to the court of Henry VIII. The Cromwells were among the select group that Belloc called "the new millionaires," the families that plundered the monasteries after Henry's split from the Catholic Church. Belloc hated this group, for in his view they attacked his church and then, under the leadership of Oliver Cromwell, used the church monies to destroy the monarchy by killing Charles. Thus, in Belloc's eyes, Cromwell was born into a tradition of ill-gotten wealth, treachery, and hypocrisy. The most interesting section of the book describes the finely orchestrated scheme by which Cromwell overcame the people's reluctance to harm their king. Cromwell trapped the unsuspecting Charles into attempting a doomed escape from prison, thus breaking down the popular sympathy for the monarch and paving the way for his trial and execution.

Up until the execution of Charles, Belloc's account of Cromwell is aloof and cold; the Puritan leader is presented as a man of limited but definite skills who succeeds in outmaneuvering the king. Once Cromwell is the undisputed ruler of England and becomes entangled in the wars against Scotland and Ireland, however, Belloc's attitude changes. Beset by financial pressures in his attempt to maintain his highly professional army, Cromwell suffers personal setbacks.

His first problem was insomnia, which "undermines the man. It strikes at the heart, diminishing its action, making irregular the blood's movement, and even sapping the will" (341). The more serious problem was the death of his daughter, which Belloc describes in this way: "Men bound up with those of their own blood can testify how, in such hours, it is the picture of the victim in childhood which returns, how living, from the past: a little child laughing in vivid light against the cloud. She had been the baby in the good quiet days before the wars had come . . ." (344). In sickness and despair, Cromwell became the vulnerable mortal that he had never been as the skilled military and political figure. Belloc was uniquely able to understand Cromwell then, for he himself was a victim of insomnia and had lost a child. Belloc's own description of his memories after his son Louis had been killed bears a remarkable resemblance to his description, years later, of Cromwell's loss: Belloc remembered "especially his [Louis's] early childhood and the days before any disasters came."[17] Through his identification with Cromwell's grief Belloc was able to transcend his hatred and write an insightful analysis of the man who killed King Charles.

While monarchy was being destroyed in England, it was reaching its greatest powers in France in Louis XIV, who dominated the seventeenth century. Belloc's book about Louis, *Monarchy: A Study of Louis XIV* (1938),[18] was a radical departure. Whereas he had stated in the introductions to all of his previous biographies that he was not attempting a traditional biography, in the case of *Monarchy* the claim was truly justified. He wrote the book because "monarchy is certainly returning after a long eclipse; its strength is already present among us, sometimes in most violent forms, and the tendency to it is working everywhere before our eyes. I have written in order to discuss and illustrate both the strength and the weakness of that institution as it appears in the capital example of Louis XIV's very great reign" (ix).

Interspersed throughout the narrative of Louis's life are speculations on the reemergence of monarchy in the modern world and even whole chapters—such as "What is Banking?"—that are only indirectly related to Louis. When riding one of his hobby horses, such as the evil of moneylenders, Belloc loses all control and restraint: "The hydra can be destroyed only by one vigorous, throttling grasp at the common root of its manifold neck" (85). Only in discussing the central drawback of monarchy—the fact that the nation is dependent on the whims of the monarch—is Belloc objective.

Despite his primary focus on the institution of monarchy, Belloc did attempt to understand the mind of the man who ruled France for over seventy years. Two aspects of Louis's life were central to Belloc. The first was his frustrated romance with Mary Mancini, who was kept from him because of her inferior rank. In describing their grand passion Belloc speaks in terms that he reserved for a description of his own marriage: "The thing has no name. For names attach only to things generally known and *this* thing, a revelation, is known to very few and is incommunicable. The only parallel to it is the experience of the mystics, their momentary union with the Divine. This, those who have been so transfigured can never later describe" (66). The second aspect of Louis's life that particularly interested Belloc was his reaction to increasing age, his attempt to maintain the glorious reign of his youth. As an old man himself, Belloc structured his study of Louis on the phases of the monarch's life:

. . . the scale of any section in human life is not measured by its years but by the intensity of its action and feeling. Louis in that early blaze was under thirty still. In the splendour of his maturity he remained till over forty. . . . But in the forties comes the turn of human life and after that change the thoughts and acts of a man rest rather on memory than on deed; and time grows less and less: it hurries to be off: after forty-five the years put on peace. Another decade and they go racing by. (16–17)

Belloc's paragraph begins as a defense of the structure of his book; it ends as a meditation on time.

Even on his deathbed Louis maintained a strict separation between his personal and official lives. His wife—who was not the queen—was forced to stand apart from "the pageantry of royal death." Through the force of his will Louis never succumbed to the temptation of weakness. He remained "in his very self the nation until the end" (389). Unlike James II of England, Louis was able to subordinate his personal goals to those of the state.

A year after *Monarchy* Belloc published *Charles II*,[19] a study of Louis XIV's first cousin. Belloc explained that his study of the English monarch was to be "a sequel and companion" to *Monarchy* (1). The crucial difference between the two reigns is that whereas the French king was able to master "the Money Power," the English king was not. *Charles II* was subtitled *The Last Rally*; the irony of Charles's reign was that he was in fact conquering the financial interests, but his early death and the coronation of his brother James led to the final capitulation of the crown in the Glorious Revolution of 1688.

The Glorious Revolution was so called because it was the non-violent installation of William and Mary as the rulers of England. Although ostensibly a religious transition—James was an avowed Catholic whereas the new rulers were Protestant—the Glorious Revolution was actually the final step in what Belloc considered the emasculation of the English monarchy.

On his deathbed Charles had accepted the Catholic faith, but all of his active life he had sacrificed his true religious inclinations to the welfare of his strongly Protestant country. For Belloc, a fervent Catholic, Charles's decision to separate his private beliefs from his public obligations represented the epitome of responsible statesmanship. Charles's devotion to the concept of monarchy was probably due to the trials of his early life. His father, Charles I, had been executed when Charles was only nineteen; during Cromwell's reign, he was constantly on the run, engaging in battle with Cromwell, fleeing to France only to be expelled later, and traveling in poverty throughout Europe.

His coronation in 1660 was celebrated by the people, but it was followed immediately by a series of grave internal and external problems. Without a source of funds, Charles faced war with the Dutch, a rebellion led by his illegitimate son Monmouth, and the always dangerous question of religious toleration. Charles's greatness, in Belloc's eyes, was his ability to manage all of the threats to his reign while simultaneously increasing England's colonial empire and greatly expanding her international trade. The growth of England's navy and maritime fleet under Charles ensured its military and economic strength.

In spite of his respect for Charles's character, Belloc is able to capture the monarch's spirit only in his love for the sea, and therefore *Charles II* lacks the sense of identification between author and subject that characterizes the other studies of monarchs. In place of the flashes of insight that brought the characters of the earlier subjects to life,

Belloc offers a reasonable but ultimately ordinary analysis of Charles. On the question of Charles's remarkable promiscuity, for instance, Belloc suggests that the almost random sexual attachments that Charles formed throughout his life had the effect of isolating him "from disturbing influences of special passions and personal appeals" (65). This comment makes sense, but it conveys none of the flavor of experience that the best of Belloc's work does. Charles II was a logical choice for his last major historical study by virtue of the crucial transformation that his early death effected, but Charles the man proved impervious to his analysis.

Belloc's studies of monarchy elicited the same critical response that all of his other histories did: praise of the forceful, evocative, and vivid style, and criticism of the biases and judgments. The sometimes virulent criticism appears not to have bothered him; he cared too little for his enemies. But the praise delighted him. And even his harshest critics agreed with the *Outlook's* review of *James the Second* : "History, in his hands, is a lively thing."[20]

Perhaps the most insightful analysis of Belloc's historical writings was Albert Leon Guerard's review of the first American edition (1928) of *Danton*: it was "an early work, and its faults were naturally ascribed to boyish immaturity. But Mr. Belloc is now nearly sixty, and he is still a boy. Need we add that nothing could make him more lovable than this perennial boyishness? At any rate, he has aspired, more daringly, perhaps, than any living writer, and he has almost attained."[21] Belloc consciously and deliberately disobeyed his elders with his provocative and unscholarly histories. Although he derived a certain amount of pleasure from his misbehavior, this posture can be attributed to a more serious cause.

Belloc had two objectives when he wrote history: to tell a good story and to tell the truth. His ability to tell a story never was disputed; his ability to tell the truth was. For Belloc, truth—a word he usually spelled "Truth"—was essentially a matter of perspective. He never thought of himself as anything other than a Catholic apologist whose task was to overstate and exaggerate his case—pro-Catholic and pro-monarchist—as a means of compensating for the Whig histories.

Another aspect of Belloc's Catholicism explains his approach to history. Just as he always distrusted documentary evidence when it violated common sense, he placed his faith in the internal coherence of a story rather than its correspondence to empirical reality. As a fervent Catholic, he accepted the faith as an imaginative act of will; he had no patience with "Bible Christians," who attempted to "prove" the scientific validity of Christian beliefs. The important truths for Belloc could not be revealed by the processes of rational analysis. They were either self-evidently true or they were not. Despite all of Belloc's justification for avoiding the scholarly techniques, he avoided footnotes because he believed that a true story does not need them.

## Chapter Four
# The Fiction

The fact that a number of Belloc's novels make interesting reading today is a testament to his native talent, for with only a few exceptions he took little interest in them, either during or after their composition. Almost all of the twenty-odd works of fiction were written quickly; most took no more than a couple of weeks. Had he chosen, he could surely have improved the quality of his novels, yet he probably would have left their content and strategy the same. Belloc was an aesthetic conservative; the novel was for him an established genre, like the sonnet, and he never thought in terms of modifying or expanding it. Except for the topicality of his subject matter, his fiction might have been written any time in the nineteenth or even the eighteenth century. Although he lived in a period that could be called the age of the novel, he ignored the more ambitious writers such as Joseph Conrad, Virginia Woolf, and James Joyce.

Belloc's attitude toward most of his fiction derived from his belief that the novel was the least demanding and least exalted of the genres. For a classicist like Belloc, epic poetry was the most noble kind of literary expression. The novel, which emerged as a popular genre as recently as the eighteenth century, was appropriate for writers who were unable to summon the time, intelligence, and magic to create poetry, and for those who needed money quickly. All that Belloc thought necessary for a novel was a thin story line and a talkative narrator. He had plenty of stories, and few writers have been able to talk as easily on so many topics. He simply paced back and forth in his study, dictating his novels.

As a result, the typical Belloc novel has an intrusive narrator and simple characterization. Unlike contemporaries such as Conrad, who often built their novels around the narrator's personality and perception, Belloc almost always used the omniscient narrator—the all-knowing teller of the tale who, more often than not, is indistinguishable from the author. And like Belloc himself, the narrator strays from the story when the mood strikes.

The characters other than the narrator usually remain two-dimensional. Whereas the modern novelists were exploring the inner recesses of their characters' sensibilities, Belloc believed that most people are essentially simple, and therefore that fictional characters could be defined adequately in a few pages. And although the characters do not always fully understand themselves, Belloc never withholds any crucial information from his readers.

Because of his approach to characterization, most of the novels follow a standard pattern. The narrator introduces a character by describing his lineage, social status, profession, physical appearance, and, finally, central personality trait. Often, Belloc presents in this way three or four characters, none of whom seems to have anything to do with any of the others. As the novel progresses, however, relationships entangle them. Eventually, all of the characters are drawn together for the climax and then the resolution of the novel.

Those who pick up a Belloc novel never forget they are reading a book. The prominent narrator prevents them from becoming too involved with any of the characters. In the more successful of the novels the characters are skillfully constructed embodiments of their primary traits, just as are the characters in a comedy of humors from the late Renaissance. In the less successful of the novels the characters are simple marionettes. Either way, Belloc was able to achieve his basic goal: to teach or amuse his readers by telling them a good story.

## The Academic Satires

Belloc's first book of prose fiction, *Lambkin's Remains* (1900), is not really a novel at all; it is a collection of articles he had written for an Oxford journal, *The J. C. R.*[1] Still living in Oxford, and bitterly disappointed at having lost the fellowship, Belloc created in Lambkin an Oxford don who represented a mixture of intellectual mediocrity and outright stupidity. *Lambkin's Remains* is a collection of the late professor's previously uncollected writings, each introduced by an obsequious editor who praises the great man's slightest effort.

In a biographical introduction to Lambkin, for example, the editor solemnly describes how the illustrious don as a child used to be bullied by "a younger and smaller, but much stronger boy" (179). "Of his undergraduate career," states the narrator reverently, "there is little to be told" (180). Lambkin would surely have won the prestigious Newdigate Prize, "had he not been pitted against two men of quite exceptional poetic gifts—the present editor of 'The Investor's Sure Prophet,' and Mr. Hound, the well-known writer on 'Food Statistics'" (180). He earned "a good Second-class in Greats" and began his thirty-year professorial career, during which "[t]here was not, of course, any incident of note . . ." (180–81).

The great care with which Lambkin wrote accounts for his small output. He regarded lucidity as the major criterion of good writing, "[a]nd if he sometimes failed to attain his ideal in this matter, the obscurity was due to . . . the fact that he found great difficulty in ending a sentence as he had begun it" (194). Nevertheless, the editor presents some of the don's great uncollected work: his illustrious heroic poem, "The Benefits Conferred by Science, Especially in Connection with the Electric Light"; his essay on the causes of sleep; his speech to the students at the end of the term—"My young friends, I have given you the pearl of great price. You have begun to doubt" (237); and his open letter to churchmen, on the question of the relative advantages and disadvantages of laced boots versus buttoned boots. Some of the professor's works are only alluded to, such as his children's book on elephant physiology, *How Jumbo is Made Inside*.

The discussion of boots is reminiscent of Swift's *Gulliver's Travels*, in which the Lilliputians in Part I classify people according to the height of the heels on their shoes. *Lambkin's Remains* has all of Swift's humor but none of his bitterness. At this point in his life Belloc was able to exorcise his bitterness through humor. Lambkin, however foolish he may be, is inconsequential. Belloc's strongest criticism of the Oxford community is not that it is evil, but that it is irrelevant. The blustering don and the dull-witted editor are a perfect pair; neither is capable of producing anything important. In his first book of fiction Belloc brought them together to create a high-spirited parody that, as one commentator noted, is worthy of Laurence Sterne.[2]

*Caliban's Guide to Letters* (1903) is Belloc's second book of prose fiction. In many ways it is similar to *Lambkin's Remains*: it is a collection of pieces Belloc had written for a newspaper (the *Speaker*); its subject is the work of an undistinguished writer (Dr. Thomas Caliban); and it consists of the writings interspersed with the editor's comments. But despite these similarities, the two parodies are quite different in tone. Whereas the earlier work employs good-natured humor, *Caliban's Guide* is more pointed and serious. Professor Lambkin remains a likeable man, despite his many limitations. Caliban, as the name suggests, is unsympathetic.

The book begins cheerfully enough, with a parodic collection of reviewers' opinions. Along with the customary vapid praise Belloc includes negative criticism, followed by the editor's rebuttal: "'. . . We found it very tedious . . .'—*The Evening German*. (The devil 'we' did! 'We' was once a private in a line regiment, drummed out for receiving stolen goods.)" (viii). As its Preface informs the reader, the book itself is meant to be a textbook for "the young aspirant to literary honors" (ix). The literary expression the book teaches, however, is basically journalism. The chapters include, for example, the review, the short story, the short lyric, the interview, and the topographical article. The two basic questions the editor addresses in describing each kind of writing are: How easy is it to do? and How much does it pay? The editor urges the reader to follow the example of Dr. Caliban, the preacher and journalist who begins his day's work at six o'clock in the evening and "write[s] steadily till seven" (14). The editor comments approvingly on Caliban's means of dealing with controversial issues, such as England's role in the Boer War: "A young radical of sorts was declaiming at his table one evening against the Concentration Camp. Dr. Caliban listened patiently, and at the end of the harangue said gently, 'Shall we join the ladies?' The rebuke was not lost" (19).

The editor's interpretation of Caliban's response to the dinner guest is humorous, but the humor is tinged with the seriousness of the subject. The Boer War was all too real, and too many people were happy to ignore the tragedy.

Once *Caliban's Guide* gets past its introduction, which describes Caliban's mental breakdown and confinement in an asylum, Belloc begins his attack on modern journalism. The best chapter, "Reviewing," teaches such practices as writing the review without having to read the book and flattering the author if his publisher buys advertising space in the newspaper. Also included is a handy list of "startling words, which lend individuality and force to the judgment of the Reviewer" (31).

The book concludes with an appendix "On Remainders and Pulping." Remainders are unsold books that are sold in bulk to the secondhand bookseller; pulping is the process of dismantling books and turning them back into blank paper. The editor affirms that England is the most patriotic country on earth, for it recirculates its literature by pulping almost three-quarters of its books: "[N]o less than 73 per cent are restored to their original character of useful blank paper within the year, ready to receive further impressions of Human Genius and to speed on its accelerated round the progress of Mankind. Amen" (159).

The reader can hear Belloc laughing at this last joke, but the laughter is filled with bitterness. By 1903 he had become a professional journalist, and *Caliban's Guide to Letters* reflects his attitude of amused disgust toward his new profession. Belloc had expected journalism to be a noble profession, for nothing could be more important than telling the public the truth. When he realized that journalism is a business, and that it therefore had its share of knaves and charlatans, he attacked it for violating a sacred trust. Only three years separated his first two books of prose fiction, but in those years his fiction had acquired its characteristic sardonic tone.

## The Political Satires

Belloc's journalistic career, and then, in 1906, his election to Parliament, gave him a firsthand understanding of the relationship between finance and politics in England. As a writer for the *Speaker* he was instrumental in publicizing the Marconi scandal, the unsavory financial dealings that enabled some national leaders to enrich themselves at the public's expense. He never forgot this incident, and as a member of Parliament he witnessed many similar occurrences.

His first sustained novel, *Emmanuel Burden* (1904), is a fictional biography of a wealthy businessman's baptism into the world of high finance. *Mr. Clutterbuck's Election* (1908), written when Belloc was serving in Parliament, shows how a businessman buys a seat in the

House of Commons. *A Change in the Cabinet* (1909) expresses the thesis that party leaders are chosen less for their abilities than for their willingness to enrich the anonymous power brokers who in fact rule Britain. *Pongo and the Bull* (1910) explores another of his favorite themes: how the excessive intimacy between the leaders of the opposing political parties frustrates the adversary relationship in a democracy and serves to maintain their own power, despite the national interest. A late work, *The Postmaster-General* (1932), completes the cycle of political novels by exploring the situation of a high-ranking government official's accepting a managerial position with a corporation that his agency regulates. Belloc's political novels thus trace a neat arc, showing how a business leader enters politics, rises to party leadership, maintains his power, and then uses it to secure a lucrative semi-retirement back in the financial community.

*Emmanuel Burden* (1904) is probably the most interesting of the group of political novels, mainly because Belloc's attitude toward the phenomenon he was analyzing is relatively complex. Unlike the four subsequent novels, in which he views the situations with unalloyed disdain, in *Emmanuel Burden* his contempt is mixed with sorrow and compassion.

Emmanuel Burden, a comfortably wealthy owner of a hardware business, is a widower with one grown son. I. Z. Barnett, an unscrupulous financier whose only passion is money, realizes that he needs to control Burden's hardware business in order to exploit the M'Korio Delta, an African region that the British have just "pacified" (64). Playing on Burden's pride, and using the devices of Burden's son, Cosmo, who is in debt, Barnett persuades the hardware merchant to enter into a syndicate to develop the M'Korio Delta. Only one more man—another merchant and a friend of Burden named Abbott—is necessary for Barnett to control all of the resources he needs to plunder the African colony. Abbott, however, knows that Barnett is unscrupulous and refuses to cooperate with the syndicate. When Burden realizes that his syndicate will not hesitate to destroy Abbott, he revolts. Burden saves his own soul, but soon dies, and his son "followed in the interests of the M'Korio, and, happily, his father did not know that he followed" (299).

Belloc's hatred of the unscrupulous world of finance is apparent as early as the Introduction, in which he adopts the mask of the biographer of Emmanuel Burden. In justifying his book, the unctuous biographer states that although he had no moral purpose in mind when he sat down to chronicle the life of Burden, he soon recognized "a Guiding Power of which I was but the Instrument. . . . [I felt] the Presence of some Mysterious Design . . . I was convinced of the Destiny of a People; I was convinced that every man who forwarded this Destiny was directly a minister of Providence" (ix—x). Like the other immoral characters in the book, the biographer is not content to be merely treacherous; he chooses to disguise his treachery behind the mask of religious sentiment.

Although Belloc hates the financiers, he views Burden with regret. In the final pages of the novel Burden is on his deathbed: "Loneliness caught him suddenly, overwhelming him; wave upon wave of increasing vastness, the boundaries leaping, more and more remote, immeasurably outwards with every slackening pulse at the temples. Then it was dark; and the Infinite wherein he sank was filled with that primeval Fear which has no name among living men: for the moment of his passage had come" (309). This scene is followed immediately by the return home of the drunken Cosmo, "after a night of pleasure with his equals" (310). The final sentence of the novel reads, "Honest Englishman and good man—I wish I could have written of him in nobler terms" (312).

This comment explains Belloc's complex attitude toward the Emmanuel Burdens of the world. At this stage in his life—he was only thirty-four years old—he believed that the fight against the well-organized forces of corruption could still be waged and, perhaps, even won. But he also believed that the naive and slow-witted, such as Burden, would always end up, however unintentionally, as accomplices to the I. Z. Barnetts. In the good fight Belloc believed that he had a role. Abbott, the honest tradesman who rejected the offers of the financiers, looks and sounds like Belloc himself. The description of Abbott includes one of Belloc's most accurate self-portraits: "As for his judgment upon any of the great complexities of modern life, no worse judge could have been discovered than this utterly simple, obstinate, loud-voiced man" (200–201). Despite Belloc's great complexities, on questions of moral behavior he saw only right and wrong.

After *Emmanuel Burden*, Belloc pictured himself as simply a commentator on the contemporary scene, not as a participant; as the conclusion of this novel testifies, the drunken Cosmo will take over his father's interests, and the forces of corruption will triumph.

The name of the title character of *Mr. Clutterbuck's Election* (1908) indicates the evolution of Belloc's thinking in the four years following the publication of *Emmanuel Burden*. Although the later novel involves a businessman's entry into the financial and political world and even employs some of the same characters that appear in the earlier book, *Mr. Clutterbuck's Election* is a simpler and less satisfying novel. Belloc at this point was more interested in sharpening his satire than in developing his characterization. By making Clutterbuck almost a caricature of Burden, he created a protagonist who would attract both the skillful and less skillful predators.

The plot concerns a comfortable but dim-witted businessman who amasses a considerable fortune and thus draws the attention of the politicians, who persuade him to run for Parliament. Despite his total ignorance of the issues, he is elected. He soon becomes a pawn in a battle between two unscrupulous antagonists and finally his election is ruled invalid. The novel ends on an ironic note: the man who ruined Clutterbuck arranges to mollify him with a baronetcy.

Belloc's purpose in *Mr. Clutterbuck's Election* was not merely to expose the techniques of corruption, for he had already done that. What he wanted to show in this novel is the calm efficiency with which the various characters carry out their manipulation of the British Empire. To convey this businesslike amorality, Belloc employs his most effective understatement. The early chapters, for instance, chronicle Clutterbuck's transformation from a successful merchant to a wealthy financier. This transformation is made possible by his own stupidity and the government's feelings of obligation to the business community. The Boer War is raging, and Clutterbuck finds himself the owner of one million eggs that he intends to sell to the government for consumption by the British soldiers. When peace is declared, Clutterbuck finds that his eggs are almost worthless. But, says Belloc in a finely understated passage,

No one recognized better than the Cabinet of the day under what an obligation they lay to the mercantile world which had seen them through the short but grave crisis in South Africa, nor did any men appreciate better than they the contract into which they virtually if not technically entered, to recoup those whom their abrupt negotiations for peace had left in the lurch. . . . the least they could do for those whose patriotism had accumulated provisions to continue the struggle, was to recompense them not only equitably but largely for their sacrifice. (29–30)

Thus Clutterbuck is paid forty-five thousand pounds for an investment of seven hundred and fifty, and Belloc makes his point effectively by simply reporting the action, without comment.

The novel, however, is not only an indictment of corrupt politicians, but also an argument that the British have the government they deserve. While Clutterbuck is reciting one of his campaign speeches written for him by his party, the ignorant townspeople in the audience completely misunderstand him, believing that he is discussing an obscure local conflict when in fact he is arguing about free-trade laws. And when election day comes, the turnout is low because of rain. Again, Belloc merely reports the action.

Belloc's movement toward sharp-edged satire at the expense of well-developed characterization continued the next year with the publication of *A Change in the Cabinet* (1909). The plot of this novel involves some influential friends of the prime minister who manipulate Parliament by having a cabinet member, from the House of Commons, elevated to the House of Lords in order to vacate his position for an incompetent acquaintance of theirs who needs the money. The acquaintance is duly elected to Parliament, by virtue of his friends' campaign contributions, and installed as the new cabinet member.

The story is fairly thin, and Belloc fleshes it out with some farce, but in places the satire redeems the novel's narrative failures. For example, in one of Belloc's great comic passages the outgoing cabinet member suffers an attack of "veracititus," an embarrassing nervous

disorder that renders the victim incapable of lying. Telling the truth
to his household servants, the members of Parliament, and the
directors of his corporation—which is currently engaged in building a
useless railroad in the wastes of Australia—the cabinet member soon
becomes a social outcast. The world of politics and finance cannot
tolerate someone who begins an address to his corporation with
"WHAT ARE WE HERE FOR? . . . MONEY!" (122) and then
proceeds to explain in exquisite detail how they will exploit their
gullible stockholders by financing the construction of a railroad for
the aborigines.

The least successful of the five political novels, *Pongo and the Bull*
(1910), shows Belloc's fatigue. He was writing these books too quickly; he had little new to say. The theme of *Pongo and the Bull* is official
collusion as the leaders of the two parties contrive to thwart the will of
Parliament. After *Pongo*, Belloc wisely decided to let the political
novel rest.

Twenty-two years later he completed his cycle of political novels
with the publication of *The Postmaster-General* (1932). Like much of
his fiction, this book is hampered by a busily episodic plot, full of too
many incidental characters. Yet *The Postmaster-General* is distinct
from the four other political novels in presenting the possibility of real
human trust and loyalty as a counterbalance to the corruption of the
political and financial world.

Belloc's familiar dupe in this novel is Wilfrid Halterton, Postmaster-General, whose problems begin when he enters into an illegal
agreement with the director of one of the country's two manufacturers
of television sets. The agreement is that Halterton is to use his
political leverage to grant the company a virtual monopoly in England in return for a lucrative contract as manager when he resigns
from government service. The plot is set in motion as the director
steals Halterton's copy of the surreptitious agreement and blackmails
him. Another cabinet minister, to whom Halterton turns for advice,
realizes an opportunity to blackmail both Halterton and the director.
Halterton's situation grows progressively more serious until at last he
is saved by a friend, Arthur Lawson.

Arthur Lawson, a Jewish immigrant born Aaron Levina, met
Halterton years before, when Jacob Levina, his younger brother, was

struck accidentally by Halterton's automobile. Lawson, who expected Halterton to flee from the scene of the accident or, at most, attempt to buy his silence, was surprised to see that Halterton was profoundly shaken by the accident, even though he hadn't been at fault, and that he pledged himself to aid the injured Jacob in whatever way possible. The Lawson brothers, who had been victims of anti-Semitic persecution in their native Lithuania, had become completely self-sufficient and mistrustful of all Gentiles. Halterton's offer was genuine, however, and he helped Jacob enter Cambridge University and obtain a well-deserved fellowship despite the anti-Semitism prevalent at the university.

Despairing at the imminent ruin of his career, Halterton asks Arthur Lawson, now a phenomenally rich financier, to help him, which he does by buying the various companies and forcing the blackmailers to turn over the incriminating evidence and to pay Halterton a large sum of money periodically until his death.

Thus concludes one of Belloc's most bizarre books. As in many of the other political novels, the status quo is maintained. Halterton is, after all, only another member of Belloc's gallery of inept rogues. But the focus of the novel is not on Halterton's corruption; indeed, if such things can be measured, he is probably less corrupt than the various blackmailers. What Belloc is saying, however, is that Halterton is basically irrelevant, for he is a man whose transgressions are so commonplace that they are hardly worth mentioning. What is extraordinary to Belloc is the depth of Lawson's commitment to the one Gentile who showed him friendship many years before.

Arthur Lawson dominates two chapters in *The Postmaster-General*, one in which Belloc tells the story of the automobile accident, and one in which Lawson promises to come to Halterton's assistance. Whereas much of the rest of the book degenerates into farce—with the incriminating documents being picked from any number of pockets—the Lawson chapters are written in an almost reverent tone. The following passage characterizes Belloc's style when discussing Lawson's commitment to Halterton:

Aaron Levina was about to do a thing as profitable to his own lonely heart as could be done. His isolation was not broken; he still remained what he had been before that brief interview [with Halterton]; but he felt that with *one* of the Goyim at least, . . . he had made a link. It mattered not. He would make no other. He was of his own people. What had he to do with the outer swarms? But he would save Wilfrid Halterton. (243)

*The Postmaster-General* is interesting in light of the frequent charges that Belloc was himself an anti-Semite; for Arthur Lawson is certainly among the few sympathetic characters in the five political novels, three of which feature Barnett, a villainous Jew. More than this, Arthur Lawson represents for Belloc the strength of personal loyalty, expressed here in the form of a shrewd and sophisticated businessman who is willing to beat the petty operators at their own game. Lawson would never be installed in Belloc's pantheon of saints, but in his devotion to Halterton he demonstrates a rare human virtue.

In his last political novel Belloc thus returned to his basic idea expressed almost three decades earlier in *Emmanuel Burden*. In that novel Burden's heroic loyalty to his friend Abbott leads to Burden's death and does nothing to stop the villains, but at least the protagonist saves his own soul. Thirty years taught Belloc that if Halterton is incapable of helping himself, an act of friendship done years earlier would bring to his assistance a master manipulator who would save at least his life.

The contemporary critical response to the five political novels focused on the question of satire and narrative. From the start, Belloc's satirical talents were recognized and applauded. The *Times Literary Supplement* for example, called *Emmanuel Burden* "one of the best sustained efforts of the mocking spirit that we have had in English."[3] The same journal wrote, in its review of *Mr. Clutterbuck's Election*, that while his satire was becoming sharper, Belloc was sacrificing the narrative elements of his novel. Whereas Burden "had qualities of greatness that commanded our respect, even our affection . . . we never admire Mr. Clutterbuck, and are never sorry for him."[4] The critical reaction to *A Change in the Cabinet* and *Pongo and the Bull* was mixed, with most readers applauding the cleverness of the satire but criticizing Belloc's redundancy in subject matter. The final political novel, *The Postmaster-General*, received strong praise for both its satire and its characterization. The *Spectator*, for example, praised

Belloc's insights into "that mad, logical world" of politics and finance.[5] And the *Times Literary Supplement* remarked on the episodes featuring the financier Lawson that the Jews "become flesh and blood, and so for a few pages does Wilfrid Halterton himself."[6]

## A Historical Novel

Belloc wrote only one historical novel, *The Girondin* (1911). It was the outgrowth of other, nonfictional studies of the French Revolution: *The French Revolution*, which he also published in 1911, and earlier biographies of Danton, Robespierre, and Marie Antoinette. The novel concerns a recruit who is a member of the Girondins, the radical wing of the revolutionaries that rallied to defend France from the invading armies of monarchist Europe.

The protagonist is Boutroux, a well-to-do young man forced to murder a fellow revolutionary who is attempting to attack the house of Boutroux's wealthy uncle. Fleeing his home and assuming a number of new identities, Boutroux falls in love with a peasant girl, is impressed into the revolutionary army, endures long and painful marches, and finally dies from injuries suffered in a riding accident.

Belloc's decision to focus on Boutroux accentuates the limitations of his fictional technique. In the political novels a large group of characters intermingle, and each character's dominant trait—whether it be greed, malice, or some personal eccentricity—advances the plot toward a resolution. Using this network of characters, Belloc concentrates on the situation, not on any one of the individual characters. In *The Girondin*, however, Boutroux is the only major character. He appears on almost every page, thus emphasizing Belloc's inadequate characterization. Boutroux is loyal to his uncle, and tired and afraid when he is marching toward war, but he shows no complexity and no development over the course of the novel. As a static character, he is on stage too long. Belloc's one attempt to give him depth—the episode in which he falls in love—is embarrassingly stilted.

In another sense, however, Boutroux's anonymity is consistent with Belloc's thesis. Although the book is titled *The Girondin*, Boutroux, like almost all of his fellow soldiers, is a reluctant recruit.

Although the Girondin leaders had some conception of their goals and their role in the revolution, the soldiers themselves, like many soldiers throughout history, were drafted into service or joined to avoid starvation. After a successful battle, for example, Boutroux learns that "there's a Republic."

"What is a Republic?" asked Boutroux.
"I don't know," said the soldier, "but it sounds bloody good!"
So he said, and he swore that he would go and drink to the Republic; and as he so swore he shambled off to where the canteen woman dispensed at an immoderate price small cups of wine from her travelling barrel on wheels. (351)

The hated monarchy might have fallen, but wine still costs too much.

Belloc is best in describing the torturous conditions of the common soldier: "like ghosts or men apart, not understanding, broken by fatigue and by the pressure of their going, went this hotch-potch of cavalry, until . . . they drooped, under a pouring rain, sodden, bewildered, meaningless, into Bar-le-Duc" (309). Belloc's battle descriptions are remarkable, especially considering that he never saw battle himself:

. . . Boutroux went back to his shelter and tried to bear the noise.
. . . when a crash so very much more abominable than all he had yet heard drove from him the memory of name and place and time. The whole fabric of the mill shivered, the air was a moment stunned and dead . . . the dreadful pause of a second, no more, was followed by a dense cloud of black and pungent smoke blowing before the high wind past either side of the building, and in the same moment came up that terrible unnumbered cry of many wounded men, shrieking and rising pointed upon a background of yet more terrible moans. He heard articulate appeals for death. . . . (346—47)

*The Girondin* is not a great novel, but it contains skillfully evocative descriptions of the French Revolution. The *Times Literary Supplement* wrote that "to deal . . . with those Titanic days and to convince is an achievement within the power, perhaps, of no one but Mr. Belloc himself."[7]

## A Romance

*Belinda* (1928) stands apart from Belloc's other novels. Whereas all of them in one way or another address the relationships among money, power, and politics, *Belinda* is his only prose treatment of the theme of romantic love. Because he put into the slim novel all he had to say on the subject, he spent eight years "changing, fitting in, adapting, dictating, erasing, spatch-cocking, caressing, softening, enlivening, glamouring, suppressing, enhancing and in general divinising" the book.[8] Belloc, who characteristically dismissed all of his writing, was tremendously proud of *Belinda*. He called it "the only piece of my writing that I have liked for more than 40 years."[9]

Set in Victorian England, the novel is a subtle combination of fairy tale and gentle satire. Belinda, a beautiful and wealthy young lady, and Horatio, a handsome but impoverished young gentleman, fall in love. An evil suitor, who wants to marry her for her dowry and eventually her inheritance, concocts a plan to make both of the lovers think they have been betrayed. Horatio sets out for Europe, to lead a nomadic existence that will help him forget his unhappy love affair. Belinda's father, meanwhile, decides that the best cure for his disconsolate daughter will be a European tour. The lovers meet in France, and, after realizing the treachery of the evil suitor, marry. Belinda's father meets the woman whom he had loved as a young man but who had been forced to marry another, richer man. Their love is revived. The evil suitor and his accomplice, an equally evil lawyer, kill each other when their plan is thwarted. Horatio and Belinda, "tried as by fire, torn asunder, rejoined, . . . attained at last to wedded felicity under an ancestral roof, until, after the brief accidents of this our mortality, they were united forever in Paradise" (188).

In creating this highly artificial plot, Belloc was attempting to direct his attention to the phenomenon of true love resisting malicious interference. By making his characters stock figures from a fairy tale, Belloc prevented them from becoming real people. The author even went so far as to emphasize his unrealistic approach to the book: when Horatio and Belinda fall in love, Belloc announces that Cupid "let fly the arrow from the bow" (23). The reader, thinking that Belloc is merely using the poet's cliché, is surprised to see Venus appear and address the two lovers: "'Pray, have you seen my Boy as you came through the wood? He wandered there with a bow and arrows for his sport, and I expect his return'" (24).

Venus is not the only mythic character to appear in *Belinda*. By alluding to doomed, tragic characters of literature, Belloc gently satirized the exaggerated passions of Horatio and Belinda. For example, the despairing Horatio, fleeing to the continent to escape his grief, is the possessed Byronic hero:

The few shepherds whom he passed in his career shrank back affrighted . . . from those eyes, too bright, that heated brow; such was his demented aspect that the very gipsies by the rare woodsides shuddered at the spectacle, and muttered charms against ill-omen as the dark horseman swept past their miserable encampments. (98–99)

And when he arrives at Dover, like Gloucester in *King Lear*, he stands poised on the cliffs, his new-found Olympian understanding the only compensation for his earthly hell.

The commentators were almost unanimously enthusiastic about *Belinda*. The *Saturday Review*, for example, wrote: "There simply is no use writing about *Belinda*, for the author has turned a lovely trick that must be witnessed at first hand. It is Mr. Belloc's bright garland at the feet of other times."[10] In one sense, this reviewer is correct in his final sentence, for Belloc believed that the previous century was a much more congenial time than the first quarter of the twentieth century, which had been blasted out of its comfortable complacency by the world war. In another sense, however, the "other times" Belloc is describing could not be measured in years. *Belinda*, like much of his poetry, was another declaration of his love for his wife, Elodie, who died fourteen years before its publication. Belinda is Elodie, and Horatio is Belloc. When Belinda's father learns from her that she is in love with Horatio, he is horrified:

"Horatio Maltravers? A beggar's brat, disreputably dragged up by a hermit? A pauper? A young beggar? An out-at-elbows fellow, a scrap and ragbag, a rotten Oxford coxcomb all curls and debts, a miserable futility . . ." (38)

*Belinda* represents Belloc's artistic re-creation of his courtship and marriage, the summit of his life.

## The Philosophical Fables

One of Belloc's favorite books was Samuel Johnson's *Rasselas*, the eighteenth-century philosophical fable about the title character's search for happiness. Whereas the purpose of a novel is usually to convey a complex vision of reality through the interplay of several developed characters, the philosophical fable develops a simple, unified vision of life. De-emphasizing the traditional techniques of fiction—characterization, dialogue, description—the writer of the philosophical fable concentrates on articulating and demonstrating a thesis. A novel is descriptive, a philosophical fable is didactic.

All of Belloc's novels are, to a degree, philosophical fables, for they all quite consciously and deliberately make a point. In addition, Belloc rarely succeeded in creating a fully developed character. A final characteristic of the philosophical fable that is evident in all of his fiction is a heavy reliance on coincidence. In a well-crafted novel the incidents seem to flow naturally and inevitably from the personalities of the characters. Belloc, however, had no interest in realistic motivations. In *A Change in the Cabinet*, for example, when he wants to introduce the comic scene in which the protagonist suffers from the attack of veracititus, Belloc simply arranges for him to receive a crack on the back of the head. The accident happens when the headrest falls off of the barber's chair in which the character is sitting; the scene is otherwise unconnected to the story. Once the character receives the blow, Belloc is free to get to his comic scene quickly.

Five of Belloc's novels in particular can be classified as philosophical fables since the manipulation of characters is highly exaggerated. One obvious technique that he uses is the intrusive narrator. In *The Man Who Made Gold* (1930), for example, a story of the moral degeneration of a chemistry professor who learns the secret of transforming lead into gold, Belloc poses the question of which of two of his characters is the more unhappy. Rather than demonstrate the answer through their actions, he simply announces, "I (being their

Creator) can search into their hearts and decide. It was the Reverend Arthur Bootle who was the more miserable" (231).

The second technique by which Belloc emphasizes his manipulation of his characters is to place them in completely alien environments. Just as Rasselas in Johnson's fable travels the world and thereby undergoes innumerable adventures, Belloc plucks his protagonists out of their everyday lives so that the reader can see how they react. In *Mr. Petre* (1925), for instance, the title character is a businessman who suddenly and inexplicably falls victim to amnesia; all he can remember is his last name. Thus, he becomes a stranger in his native London. In *The Green Overcoat* (1912) a psychology professor is about to walk home after a party when he realizes his overcoat is missing. The Devil encourages him to "borrow" a beautiful green overcoat, and he vows to send it back as soon as he gets home. On the way home, however, he is kidnapped by two young men who are waiting for the owner of the green overcoat. In this way Belloc removes his professor from his comfortable, orderly university world. Like the chemistry professor in *The Man Who Made Gold* and the businessman in *Mr. Petre*, the psychologist is forced to define himself.

Two of Belloc's philosophical fables—*The Hedge and the Horse* (1936) and *The Mercy of Allah* (1922)—deserve special mention. The former is distinct from the other books in that it offers an uncharacteristically complex resolution; the latter is distinct because of its bitter and sardonic thesis.

The title of *The Hedge and the Horse* is a reference to the English proverb about how some persons are more lucky than others: "One man may steal a horse and another mayn't look over a hedge." In the novel the first man is represented by Bill Robinson, a suave manipulator who is never without women or money. His opposite is Wilfred Straddle, a hapless innocent who is constantly taken advantage of by his friend Bill.

The central character, however, is Belloc himself, or at least his highly intrusive narrator. Often he will interrupt his story to comment on the action:

I think . . . [Wilfred] . . . should have been grateful to . . . [Bill] . . . for the excitements that were to follow. We ought to be grateful, surely, for the downs as well as the ups. Both are movement; and all movement is fun. And Wilfred Straddle, like Ulysses, was to know many places and men, many adventures. . . . you shall hear all about that, if God spares my life and reason to finish this book, and gives you the strength to read it. (59)

Whatever busy and complicated actions occur in the novel are just part of the grand comic plan: "I think it has something to do with some woman or other who ate apples long ago in Mesopotamia" (12). Despite Belloc's repeated warnings—"doing your duty on this earth in any form, from punctuality to patriotism, only brings disaster" (67)—both Wilfred and Bill meet kind fates. Wilfred marries a good woman and inherits a large sum of money, and Bill—what else? —enters politics: "It had been impossible, of course, to keep him out of the Cabinet" (299).

This may appear to be a simplistic conclusion, but, as always with Belloc, the statement is more complex than it seems. Ironically, in a novel in which the narrator does so much talking, the main point remains implicit. The "hedge and horse" proverb is false. Wilfred and William are separate characters only in fiction. In fact, they are the complementary halves of the same person. Each person struggles to reconcile the twin impulses of good and evil. Belloc had no interest in tying up the loose ends of his two characters, and so he assigned them a happy conclusion. The struggle, however, remains; it all has to do with that woman who ate apples.

*The Mercy of Allah* is a satirical attack on capitalism, and especially the institution of usury. The political novels include rogues such as I. Z. Barnett, the unscrupulous usurer, but *The Mercy of Allah* is Belloc's first book devoted exclusively to the evils of capitalism. Mahmoud, the protagonist, is reprehensible to Belloc because he is not content merely to take advantage of everyone he meets; like the character of the biographer of *Emmanuel Burden*, he justifies his actions by reference to a higher authority. In Mahmoud's case, that authority is Allah. Two things lead to great wealth: "the unceasing appetite to snatch and hold from all and at every season . . . [and] . . . that profound mystery, the Mercy of God" (5).

Mahmoud is a wealthy Arab merchant who gathers his nephews around him every week to explain to them how he became the man he is. Each chapter is the story of another scheme, some of which fail, most of which succeed. One chapter, for instance, "The Bridge," describes how he destroys the business of a ferry operator by buying a fleet of ferries and undercutting his price. With the ferry operator out of the way, Mahmoud builds a bridge and collects a heavy toll. Finally, he converts the toll into a tax, by which he earns a formidable income.

In other chapters he explains how as a statesman he introduced the concept of paper money and deficit spending, and how he invented loan sharking and insurance. Through irresponsible business practices he ruined his country by making the upper classes decadent and lower classes slothful, but he escaped unscathed. While he is explaining his wisdom to his nephews—"it is wealth and wealth alone . . . that can procure . . . that profound content which furnish[es] for the heart of man its resting place . . ."—one of them tricks him into signing a withdrawal slip. Realizing that this one boy has fully understood his lesson, Mahmoud wills to him all of his estate.

The critical reception of the philosophical fables was mixed. The *Saturday Review*, for instance, wrote that *The Mercy of Allah* is "altogether a finer achievement than Mr. Belloc's earlier political satires";[11] at the same time the *Times Literary Supplement* declared that Belloc is "not quite so witty nor nearly so plausible as in the brave days of *Mr. Clutterbuck's Election*."[12]

## The Farces

In the last four years of the 1920s Belloc wrote four novels that might best be described as farces. While he continued to satirize his favorite victims—corrupt businessmen, politicians, journalists, and moneylenders—the strategy of these works is different from that of the other novels. Like most of his fiction, the farces are built around the moral flaws of the characters. But the farces are characterized by an emphasis on wildly improbable slapstick. The characters' morality serves merely as the starting point, not the end, of Belloc's farces. In *The Emerald of Catherine the Great* (1926), for instance, the expensive jewel turns up missing at a country-house gathering, and each of the guests fears that he is a suspect. A kitchen boy finds the emerald, but afraid that he will be punished for having stolen it, he deposits it in the pocket of one of the guests. The emerald gets passed from one guest's pocket to another; nobody wants to explain how he got his hands on it.

*The Haunted House* (1927) is representative of the farces in that it shows the fate of Belloc's attempts to be frivolous and carefree. The story is hopelessly thin. Henry Maple, owner of a small ancestral estate but utterly lacking any professional skill, is forced to borrow substantial sums from his businessman brother in order to keep the estate solvent. Both brothers eventually die, but the businessman's widow manages to wrest control of the estate from Henry's only heir, his son John. The plot concerns John's attempts to buy the estate back from his unscrupulous aunt, who has put it up for sale at a hefty price. John's scheme involves scaring away the prospective buyers of the estate by convincing them that it is haunted. This he accomplishes using his skills as a professional ventriloquist. When the interested parties flee from the haunted house, John buys it for the amount his father had borrowed from the brother.

Belloc attempted to enliven this little story in the manner of P. G. Wodehouse. The highly unbelievable plot is reminiscent of Wodehouse, as is some of the dialogue, such as this passage between John and his intelligent girlfriend, Bo:

> Bo leant forward and spoke in a lower voice.
> "You remember Aunt Hilda wanting a ghost at Rackham, and how you told me and how angry you were? This winter? Just after you'd left her?"
> "Yes," said John, "I can't bear to think of it."
> Bo lowered her voice almost to a whisper.
> *"We'll haunt 'em!"* she said to him. "We'll haunt 'em good and hard—and *then*, Jacko," she leant back again with a conquering smile on her face, *"then* Rackham's yours for the asking." (101)

But Belloc's cheerfulness is largely hollow. The disappearance of traditional England, the growth of the usurers, the corruption of the newspapers, and the buying of honors and privilege—these and other themes in the novel remained serious issues in Belloc's mind, and no amount of verbal pretense could hide his real attitude. As the *Spectator* put it, ". . . alas, Mr. Belloc is not good-humored; he writes with scorn."[13] Here, for example, in a characteristic passage, the narrator explains why Aunt Hilda is feverishly making alterations to her newly acquired estate:

Had John Maple known more of the world, and wholly lost his innocence, he could have answered, as you and I can answer, that there are only two explanations of such feverish changes, when an old house is pulled about and made vulgar. Either the Vandal has more money to spend than she knows what to do with, or the Goth is embarrassed. Either the barbaric hand is filled with the ruining gold, or the savage heart is tortured by perpetual demands for payment from creditors and is salting for a sale. (81)

Belloc really disliked Aunt Hilda and all that she represented; no amount of forced cheerfulness could disguise that.

The evolution of Belloc's outlook on life is reflected in his fiction. After his first real novel, *Emmanuel Burden*, he could rarely sustain a sympathetic identification with his subject. Except for *Belinda* and *The Girondin*, the novels show Belloc's increasing sense of aloofness. In the political novels this distancing increases the sharpness of the satire while weakening the other aspects of the fiction. But in the farces Belloc's distancing adds a disturbingly clinical coldness. When he realized that his political novels had no more practical effect on the establishment than any of his other writing did, he tried to transform his satiric vision into a comic one. Yet Belloc could emulate P. G. Wodehouse—whom he called the greatest living writer in English[14]—no more successfully than he could have emulated James Joyce. He could mimic the technique, but the result was all wrong. Fiction was not Belloc's natural medium; only when he was totally engaged by his subject—the French Revolution, idealized romance, and a financier who he hoped would maintain his integrity—could he engage his readers.

## Chapter Five

# The Essays

In an essay entitled "A Conversation with a Reader" Belloc describes an encounter on a train with a man who is reading one of "my too numerous books of essays."[1] Unaware that he is talking to the author, the man tosses down the book, disgusted, and complains to Belloc that the book lacks coherence and a plot: "There's no story I can make out. It's all cut up." Belloc thinks to himself sadly that the man is right, that the book is merely a collection of "newspaper articles which I, poor hack, had strung together, and put between covers for my living." The man gets off at the next station after having sold his book to its author for a few pennies. Flipping through the collection, Belloc thinks:

[R]eading a sentence here and a phrase there, I was disgusted. What with affectation in one place and false rhetoric in another and slipshod construction in a third and a ghastly lack of interest in all, I wished from the depths of my soul that I had never made myself responsible for the thing at all. Then my misery was added to by the sudden recollection that it would be my duty, that very week, to gather together yet another sheaf of such chance articles and put them again between covers . . .[2]

Belloc was exaggerating his misery, of course, for comic effect, but it is probably true that he never would have written a single essay had he not needed money. His essays are distinct from his other kinds of writing in one major respect: they are the only product that he consistently was able to sell twice. First, he sold them to newspapers. Then, when he had enough for a book, he sold them to a publisher. In sum, he wrote over four hundred essays. He often composed two or three in an afternoon to break up the drudgery of a more difficult project. Because they are brief and their range of subjects is limitless, the essay was in a sense the perfect form for him.

The informality of Belloc's approach to his collections is suggested by a few of the titles: *One Thing and Another*, *This and That*, and *On Nothing*. Sometimes he simply used the title of the first essay in the collection, and he rarely attempted to unify his collections thematically.[3] A typical collection such as *On*, for example, includes essays on the following topics: bad verse, how to convince people, mumbo-jumbo, inaccuracy, the accursed climate, Exmouth, a piece of rope, and the word *and*.

## Belloc's Concept of the Essay

As Belloc's work habits would suggest, the essays themselves are highly informal.[4] Although many of them are serious and a number are beautifully delicate, the bulk are intended as light entertainment. The first person pronoun predominates, and the best of the essays sound as if Belloc is simply talking. Most are not structured logically but according to the pattern of associations in Belloc's mind; the digression is one of his favorite techniques. The essay "On Cheeses," for instance, begins with this paragraph:

If antiquity be the test of nobility, as many affirm and none deny (saving, indeed, that family which takes for its motto "Sola Virtus Nobilitas," which may mean that virtue is the only nobility, but which may also mean, mark you, that nobility is the only virtue—and anyhow denies that nobility is tested by the lapse of time), *if*, I say, antiquity be the only test of nobility, then cheese is a very noble thing.[5]

This paragraph leads into a digression on the subject of digressions, covering such topics as how to punctuate algebra, Belloc's view of a certain journalist, and Dr. Johnson. Finally, some five hundred words into his essay on cheese, he writes:

And now to cheese. I have had quite enough of digressions and of follies. They are the happy youth of an article. They are the springtime of it. They are its riot. I am approaching the middle age of this article. Let us be solid upon the matter of cheese.[6]

Because of the wide variety of styles and subjects included in each collection, the evolution of Belloc's handling of the essay is obscured.

Whereas any single collection of essays is likely to include all of his styles and moods, the earlier books are more open and enthusiastic, the later ones darker and more bitter.

In an attempt to survey the range of Belloc's essays, this chapter considers six of his favorite modes: metaphysical, satirical, elegiac, literary critical, comic, and historical.

## The Metaphysical Essays

In "The Looe Stream," an essay included in his first collection, *Hills and the Sea* (1906),[7] Belloc is writing of how experience at sea broadens a man. He would like to examine this topic, "but if one once began on this, one would be immeshed and drowned in the metaphysical, which never yet did good to man nor beast" (162). As a man who liked clear and specific explanations for what he saw around him, Belloc was suspicious of metaphysics, the study of first principles and ultimate reality. Metaphysics implied for Belloc a sterile, abstract intellectual exercise, a kind of selfish introspection.

Paradoxically, few men were more interested in first principles and ultimate reality than Belloc was. Although he never would have used the term, metaphysical essays fill *Hills and the Sea*. In writing these essays, Belloc wanted to describe the process of attaining transcendental awareness. Yet he believed that this profound sensitivity was possible only through a physical separation from humanity and a strenuous encounter with the natural world. The world beyond the senses could be viewed exclusively through the senses.

*Hills and the Sea* is in fact structured around the metaphysical essay. Unlike any of Belloc's other collections of essays, *Hills and the Sea* begins with a kind of preface, in which he describes how two men used to travel together, in the mountains and on a small boat, singing songs and performing marvelous deeds of courage and daring. The two men, however, are now dead. "They will never again be heard . . . singing their happy songs: they will never more drink with their peers in the deep ingle-nooks of home. They are perished. They have disappeared" (xiv—xv). To record their adventures, Belloc writes, this book was put together. "And there is an end of it."

These two men are Belloc and a friend, Phil Kershaw, who did in fact travel together extensively. By describing their exploits in the form of tall tales, Belloc was approaching as close as he felt comfortable to the statement that the physical adventures he and Kershaw shared had metaphysical implications.

In "The Channel" Belloc describes the physical adventures as an attempt to "find what the men who made us found, and to see the world as they saw it," to experience "the freshness of beginnings . . ." (196). By blocking off the rational faculties—the reading, writing, and thinking—and approaching the physical world primitively, as in a walking tour or an ambitious sail in a small boat, one can hope to become receptive to transcendent insights and make them a permanent part of his character. Going to sea in a small boat, for example, one "learns terror and salvation, happy living, air, danger, exultation, glory and repose at the end; and they are not words to him, but, on the contrary, realities which will afterwards throughout his life give the mere words a full meaning" (197).

In "The Inn of the Margeride," a travel essay about a walking tour in France, Belloc offers an explicit statement of the rewards of mountain climbing:

It is as though humanity were permitted to break through the vulgar illusion of daily sense, and to learn in a physical experience how unreal are all the absolute standards by which we build. It is as though the vast and the unexpected had a purpose, and that purpose were the showing to mankind in rare glimpses what places are designed for the soul—those ultimate places where things common become shadows and fail, and the divine part in us, which adores and desires, breathes its own air, and is at last alive. (57)

The experience of mountain climbing enables a person to create an enlightened definition of reality.

The most ambitious of the metaphysical essays is "The Wing of Dalua," in which the author's speculations grow naturally out of the realistic narration and remain tantalizingly mysterious. Belloc and Kershaw, described as the Two Men from the preface, set out on their adventure because they "had revealed to them by their Genius a corner of Europe wherein they were promised more surprises and delights than in any other" (31). High in the Andorra region of the Pyrenees, the two are assaulted by a storm "set in order by some enemy to ruin us . . ." "An infernal thunder, . . . great useless and blinding glares of lightning," and huge hailstones "leaping from the bare rocks like marble" combine with a rain that seems forced through a hose under great pressure. The storm finally subsides, but the two men soon realize that it had been "but the beginning of an unholy adventure. We had been snared into Fairyland" (38). A passage such as the following conveys the flavor of Belloc's writing:

[W]ith every step downward we were penetrated more and more with the presence of things not mortal and of influences to which any desolation was preferable. At one moment voices called to us from the water, at another we heard our names, but pronounced in a whisper so slight and so exact that the more certain we were of hearing them the less did we dare to admit the reality of what we had heard. (39)

When they see a man before them, they extend their hands, but touch only "a rough and silent stone." After a long sleep in a cave, the two awake simultaneously into the world they had left. They see people and hear a nearby church bell. Their strange adventure has led them back to where they had begun, but their trip down the face of the mountain had brought them through uncharted territory: "No men except ourselves have seen it, and I am willing to believe that it is not of this world" (43).

"The Wing of Dalua" stands apart from Belloc's other metaphysical essays because its narrative actually demonstrates the characters' thoughts rather than just reporting them. The readers participate in an exciting experience and thus gain a more accurate impression of Belloc's idea. The story conveys a sense of an exotic other world without reducing it to a simple metaphor. Belloc keeps his readers enchanted by the skill of his description and leaves them with a satisfying but unresolved conclusion. Like Coleridge's "The Rime of the Ancient Mariner," "The Wing of Dalua" is in the finest tradition of the Christian ghost story that suggests far more than it says.

## The Satirical Essays

The essay provided the most natural vehicle for Belloc's satires. In an essay he could speak in his own voice or create a narrative or an allegory. Sometimes, in fact, he wrote miniature dialogues between,

for instance, two politicians. The fact that the essay form requires
only a few pages enabled Belloc to create sharp-edged satires without
having to concern himself with such matters as character development. Satires of literature, morality, religion, fashion, and dozens of
other topics appear throughout all of his essay collections. Political
satires form the largest category, however, and they are clustered
most dramatically in the collection *On Nothing* (1908).

At the time of the publication of *On Nothing* Belloc was a disgrun-
tled member of Parliament. He felt absolutely no party loyalty, and
therefore the political satires are nonpartisan. In "On Jingoes: In the
Shape of a Warning," for instance, Belloc returns to his favorite
theme of collusion between the two major parties. He calls the two
parties Hocus and Pocus; the party leaders, however, refer to themselves as Freedom and Glory:

Now Freedom and Glory . . . put it to each other that, as their master was
evidently mad it would be a thousand pities to take no advantage of it, and
they agreed that whatever bit of jobbing Hocus Freedom should do, Pocus
Glory should approve; and contrariwise about. But they kept up a sham
quarrel to mask this . . . (168–69)

"On Jingoes" is a synopsis of Belloc's political theory that England
had degenerated since the replacement of a strong monarchy by a
weak republic. John Bull foolishly ceded his power to his son, Jack,
who pursued short-sighted domestic and foreign policies until at last
"he came to selling tokens of little leaden soldiers" for a living. In
other essays in *On Nothing* Belloc addresses the specific policies that
impoverished the nation.

The folly of colonial expansion is the subject of "On a Man who was
Protected by Another Man." The protected man is Mahmoud, a
desert dweller who lived an uneventful but amiable nomadic life.
When he needed something, such as a new tent or camel, he would go
down to the sea and "hoick out a pearl." The protector is Smith: "He
did not keep his word particularly; and he was exceedingly fond of
money" (137). In exchange for Mahmoud's pearls, Smith gives him
goods from his bag of great wealth. Smith's purpose in coming to the
desert is to "protect" Mahmoud, who placidly agrees, not knowing
what "protection" means. In a thinly veiled allusion to Rudyard

Kipling, Belloc writes that the bored Smith "wrote poetry about himself, making out Mahmoud to be excessively fond of him.'¹ But Mahmoud's failure to appreciate this poetry leads Smith to change his theme: his new poetry shows Mahmoud "to be a villain and a serf" and Smith "to be under a divine mission."

The relationship between the two men breaks down when Mahmoud begins running around outside his tent, "waving his hands in the air, and shouting incongruous things. . . . and firing off his gun and calling upon his god" (139). To Smith, this inexplicable behavior amounts to a breach of trust. Exhausted after his religious observance, Mahmoud refuses to get more pearls for Smith, who then returns home.

Belloc's simple allegory of British imperialism is chillingly prophetic. It conveys, first, the recognized fact that the industrialized nations plundered the natural resources of the colonies and sowed there an acquisitiveness that had not existed before. In addition, however, it shows that neither of the two peoples made an adequate attempt to understand the cultural differences that separated them. This blindness, expressed as Mahmoud's placid misunderstanding of capitalism and Smith's revulsion when he witnesses Mahmoud's religious exercise, leads to the final disagreement.

In addition to causing bloodshed and hatred, imperialism placed a tremendous strain on the English economy. "On National Debts" is Belloc's satirical attack on deficit spending. The essay is based on the proverb about robbing Peter to pay Paul. Peter, the poor young man, represents England; Paul, fantastically rich, is the financial community. They live together in a set of bare rooms, which Peter wants Paul to improve. "To all this Paul listened doubtfully, pursing up his lips, joining the tips of his fingers, crossing his legs and playing the solemn fool generally" (145). Paul persuades the dull-witted Peter to agree to an alternative to paying cash for new furnishings: "I will *lend* the whole sum of ten pounds to our common stock and we will each pay one pound a year as interest to myself for the loan" (146). The inevitable occurs. Peter borrows more and more from Paul, until finally he is borrowing just to keep up with the interest payments. Paul watches the helpless Peter starve to death.

The story does not end there. Once he has lost his benefactor, Paul realizes that "within a short time I shall be compelled to work for my living!" Faced with this dismal prospect, Paul takes his own life. Belloc's sardonic consolation is that in destroying England, the moneylenders will at least destroy themselves.

Throughout the political essays in *On Nothing* Belloc showed the simultaneous repulsion and attraction that characterized all satirists. His tone was bitter and scornful, and his stories were apocalyptic, yet his diatribes were motivated by a sincere desire to cleanse his country by purging it of its poisons. In an essay entitled "On a Hermit whom I knew" Belloc provides a kind of self-portrait. Dramatizing himself as the hermit living in a cave on the hill above the city, he writes:

My contemplation . . . is this wide and prosperous plain below: the great city with its harbour and ceaseless traffic of ships, the roads, the houses building, the fields yielding each year to husbandry, the perpetual activities of men. I watch my kind and I glory in them, too far off to be disturbed by the friction of individuals, yet near enough to have a daily companionship in the spectacle of so much life. (204)

Distancing himself from his beloved England by means of the satirical essays, Belloc was able to proclaim what it might become and hope to contribute in some small way to its improvement.

## The Elegiac Essays

Belloc never quite became that hermit. Even though he always portrayed himself looking down on the busy world from an Olympian perspective, he could not resist an active pursuit of a just society. Belloc's last essays show no decrease in his enthusiasm for reform.

When Belloc reached the middle years of his life, however, a part of him turned away from the constant struggle. He began to speculate on the broader question of human existence: what does the world do to the soul of man? In what might be called his elegiac essays, he attempted to isolate what was lost and what could be gained. *On Something* (1910) contains a representative selection of these essays.

The term *elegy* of course suggests loss and death. When he spoke openly about life, Belloc was almost uniformly melancholy and conscious of death even when he was only forty, before his personal tragedies. "The Portrait of a Child," a meditation inspired by a photograph of a young girl at play, is a beautiful statement of his awareness of loss.

Addressing the young girl directly, Belloc speculates on her future:

[Y]our little hands . . . will grasp most tightly that which can least remain . . . and will caress that which will not respond to the caress. Your eyes, which are now so principally filled with innocence that that bright quality drowns all the rest, will look upon so much of deadly suffering and of misuse in men, that they will very early change themselves in kind; and all your face . . . will grow drawn and self-guarded, and will suffer, some agonies, a few despairs, innumerable fatigues, until it has become the face of a woman grown. (236)

The sorrow of childhood for Belloc was, as it was for Gerard Manley Hopkins in "Spring and Fall," that the world will destroy its innocence. The sacred spirit that effortlessly inhabits the child must be crushed: "It is the character of whatever is sacred that . . . like a true victim, [it] remains to the end, ready to complete the sacrifice" (238).

The next essay in the collection, "On Experience," outlines the process by which the world kills the innocent. The phase of youth ends, often abruptly:

It is not the first death, perhaps .. . . . nor the first loss—no, not even, perhaps, the first discovery that human affection also passes. . . . One death, one change, one loss, among so many, unseals his judgment, and he sees thenceforward, nay, often from one particular moment . . . the doom which lies upon all things whatsoever that live by a material change. (245)

The mature man, now aware that he is doomed, spends his time seeking out friends and the beautiful objects of the world. "The equilibrium of his soul is only to be discovered in marching and continually marching. He now knows that he must go onward, he may not stand, for if he did he would fall" (247).

In the final phase—old age—man can find wisdom. He can tell the world "that though all things human pass, all bear their fruit" (248). Even though as we look around us we see nothing but misery, nothing that can equal the glories of our music, our art, our gods, these all will be replaced. "Out of dead passages [will spring] up suddenly, and quite miraculously, whatever was thought to be lost" (249).

Belloc knew, however, that age does not automatically confer wisdom. If a man does not achieve "this sort of clear maturity of spirit . . . [he succumbs to] either despair or folly, or an exaggerated shirking of reality, which, being a falsehood, is wickeder than despair, and far more inhuman than mere foolishness" (247). He becomes avaricious or unrealistic. Most often, he will not face the fact that the world and everything in it are transitory. He falls into a "sterile" regret for the past.

When Belloc wrote these words he was still in the second phase of his own life. As he admitted, "What this third phase is I confess I do not know, and as I have not felt it I cannot describe" it (247). The sad irony of his life is that in this one important instance he prophesied all too accurately. Rarely was he to experience the serenity he had described; most often, he lived his later years regretting what time had done to his world. His essay demonstrates perhaps the essential truth about wisdom: it cannot be taught, even by the best of teachers, and sometimes it cannot even be learned.

## The Literary Critical Essays

Belloc's attitude toward literary criticism is suggested by his comment, "Of all fatiguing, futile, empty trades, the worst, I suppose, is writing about writing."[8] Belloc produced relatively little literary criticism in his career: *Avril*, a book of essays on French Renaissance poets; a critical biography of Milton; an appreciation of his friend G. K. Chesterton; and an essay on translation. Perhaps because his own reading habits were so eccentric—he freely admitted his ignorance of most contemporary literature—he felt unqualified to write serious criticism. Certainly he considered literary criticism basically irrelevant: if the literature is good, what need is there for an interpretation or analysis?

In his essays, however, Belloc felt free to discuss writers he had just discovered, or those whom he reread constantly. He also put down his thoughts on the different genres, particularly poetry. And often he turned his attention to the trials and satisfactions of the life of the professional writer. *Short Talks with the Dead* (1926) contains a representative sampling of his critical essays.

"Talking of Byron" characterizes his style—and his major weakness as a critic. Like most poets who comment on other poets' work, Belloc imposed the standards he himself followed. Thus, he felt no need to justify his argument that a poet is successful to the extent that he demonstrates the virtues of classicism. And he rarely restrained himself in castigating what he saw as the debased modern spirit of literature. For example, Byron "never lapses into those two vile weaknesses with which our moderns are paralytically possessed: the itch for mere emotion and the impotence of obscurity" (35). Belloc praised Byron for his intelligence, the "magic" of his word choice, and his consistency.

Other commentators have isolated these same qualities in Byron; the assessment is reasonable. The problem, however, is that it is not reasoned; that is, Belloc failed to structure a developed, substantiated argument. Just as he avoided the scholarly conventions in his historical studies, he neglected to exemplify his generalizations. For instance, Belloc writes that "Byron perpetually strikes the note of experience: the experience of men living as the English of his time mostly lived. . . . He struck or recalled or evoked the emotions of men to whom a mechanical industrial life was either unknown or imperfect or irksome" (33). But what exactly does Belloc mean by "the note of experience"? A brief annotated quotation from Byron would clarify the point. The frustration of reading Belloc's criticism is that it appears tantalizingly perceptive, but it rarely fulfills its promise. A casual comparison between Byron and Shelley, for instance, suggests that Belloc was highly perceptive as a reader— despite his biases and prejudices: "When Shelley wrote: 'I arise from dreams of thee,' he wrote something with more lift in it, perhaps, than Byron ever managed, and certainly with more subtlety of rhythm. But the long efforts of Shelley are full of balderdash" (36). Most readers of the Romantic poets would probably agree with Belloc intuitively and want to hear more. But that is all he has to say about Shelley.

In making his point about Byron's consistency, Belloc held up as a contrast Wordsworth, who "never wrote even a sonnet, let alone a longer piece, in which there are not the most damnable break-downs—like an athlete sitting on the floor exhausted in the midst of his performance" (36). This is a striking simile, but again he did not elaborate.

However, in another essay in the same collection, "We are Seven," Belloc demonstrated that if he chose to get specific he could write informative—and witty—literary criticism.

"We are Seven" is a parodic attack on Wordsworth's ballad of that title. Belloc exemplifies Wordsworth's "damnable breakdown" by contriving a man whose hobby is to test great poetry by seeing whether he can improve individual lines:

He used his regular critical apparatus (as he loved to call it); writing down the four lines in large block letters upon a piece of good handmade paper eight inches by five inches, learning them by heart, setting them about fifteen inches from his eyes, then . . . attempting his first variations:

> A simple child, dear brother Jim,
> That lightly draws its breath,
> And feels its life in every limb,
> What should it know of death?                    (120)

The man is stymied: these four lines are "the summit of human expression in their own sphere" (121). But, Belloc adds, his friend does try to improve the quatrain: "Would that I had room for the whole series, the permutations and combinations of which came to over six hundred examples" (121). Some of the emendations are good, but "manifestly inferior to the original":

> A simple child, dear brother Jack,
> That lightly draws its breath,
> And feels its breath all down its back, etc.

> A simple child, dear brother Joe,
> That lightly draws its breath,
> And feels its life in every toe, etc.

In isolating the third line of Wordsworth's quatrain and "proving" that it cannot be improved, Belloc is of course saying just the opposite: it is a perfectly ordinary and undistinguished line that impresses only those whose hobby is to rewrite great poetry. Such an essay makes no attempt to be fair: the serious criticism levelled against Wordsworth could be applied to any poet, including Belloc. But "We are Seven" is good fun.

In addition to writing about authors who upheld or violated his own critical principles, Belloc wrote highly personal appreciations of those whose works exemplified his own burdens and dilemmas. In "Talking of Livy," for instance, he focuses his comments on Livy's tremendous output. Like Belloc, Livy "must have dictated":

This man Livy (I am beginning to grow enthusiastic) shovelled out work by the ton. . . . Take heart, therefore, you my fellow hacks, and when men jeer at you for writing and still writing, answer over your right shoulder: "Livy," and turn to the task again. (41)

Livy, too, was criticized for writing inaccurate history: "In this, therefore, Livy is our brother, for he also is subject to being set right by dwarfs and to suffering the fantasies of fools" (43). Belloc concludes his essay with the wish that when he meets Livy "on the far side of the Ferry, this suffering at the hands of fools may be a sufficient bond between us . . ." (43–44).

Belloc's best essay on literature is "Rasselas," in which he combines the objective and personal modes of criticism. Reaffirming a central precept of its author, Samuel Johnson, Belloc argues that in a comparison of *Rasselas* with Voltaire's *Candide*, a similar contemporary work, the reader must remember that a work of art should not be judged solely on its artistic merit: "There is also the prime question whether the book be noble or ignoble, moral or immoral, whether it does us good or harm" (175). Accordingly, in a sentence whose balanced phrasing recalls Johnson's style, Belloc asserts: "No good man is the better for having read *Candide*, but every man is the better for having read *Rasselas*" (175). After quoting and analyzing an excerpt from the marriage debate in *Rasselas*, he concludes: "I would maintain upon this long extract . . . that it has these four qualities—What it says is (1) true, (2) important, (3) of good moral effect, and (4) packed" (176).

The personal part of the essay on *Rasselas* discusses two main topics: Belloc's identification with Johnson as a professional writer, and his appreciation of a valuable annotated copy of the fable. Calling himself "a humble colleague of that great man, being myself a hack writer," Belloc applauds Johnson's having written the book quickly for a good sum, and then having received a bonus from the publisher "when he saw the thing selling." The valuable copy of *Rasselas* that Belloc describes was owned by Mrs. Piozzi, a woman whose family provided company and a second home for Johnson in his later, lonely years. In discussing her annotated copy Belloc wanted only to share with his readers the comments written by Mrs. Piozzi, in her final days, about the great man whom she knew so well. The essay concludes with a reference to her comment on Johnson's sentence, "What is to be expected from our pursuit of happiness, when we find the state of life to be such that happiness itself is the cause of misery?" Belloc writes, "to this the old woman's shaking fingers add, *'Oh melancholy truth, to which my heart bears witness.'* And after that comes only a long quavering line" (183). Despite the unorthodoxy of his critical methods, Belloc was particularly effective in fulfilling one of the goals of literary criticism: he could convey his enthusiasm and reverence for great literature.

## The Comic Essays

Belloc was often a high-spirited man, and his friends referred time and again to his capacity for buoyant and uninhibited frivolity. Over the years, his humor became bitter and cynical, but he never lost his lighter comic touch. In addition to his satires, Belloc wrote dozens of comic essays that have no serious point at all. A later volume, *A Conversation with an Angel* (1928), contains a number of comic essays that suggest the author's range and strategy.

In an essay on the comedy of academic debates Belloc offers a basic definition of humor: "All things are funny which are out of proportion" (28). Like most humorists, he knew better than to attempt a more specific definition, for he realized that most humor defies analysis. In an essay "On Laughter," a response to Lord Chesterfield's advice that audible laughter is unsophisticated, Belloc provides the following definition: "Note it carefully; indeed, you will do well to write it down. Genuine laughter is the physical effect produced in the rational being by what suddenly strikes his immortal soul as being damned funny. This is a first-rate definition" (92).

This beautifully circular definition demonstrates one of Belloc's favorite devices for humor on a small scale: the noble introduction undercut by a humble conclusion. On one page of his essay "On Not Reading Books" Belloc uses the technique twice. One example apparently compliments modern writers: "They can get right into the souls of people who do not interest me." The other example praises book reviewers: "I confess to a very sincere admiration of my friends who review novels. I know, quite intimately, at least five men who review novels (if I may say so respectfully) in the bulk; as men scrape fish in a fish shop" (249). Sometimes Belloc reverses the standard sequence of the big and little elements to produce his laugh. In the essay "On the Fall of Lucifer" he is speculating on a painting that he read was eight feet by four feet:

I am taking it for granted that "The Fall of Lucifer" is tall rather than long. . . . It seems common sense that he should fall downwards, like anybody else. So I take it that somewhere in the world there exists this glorious thing, about as big as a French window or the chassis of a Rolls-Royce, and representing what I, for my part, regard as the best moral story in the world, showing the consequences of misuse in the matter of freewill. (59)

In addition to this kind of verbal humor, Belloc was adept at situational humor: an idea whose comic potential derives from its inappropriateness in a particular context. The essay "On Pavement Artists" describes how the men who draw chalk portraits on London sidewalks always add "some simple statement of their right to attention. Sometimes they tell us that the work is wholly their own; sometimes they are married and have a family; sometimes that they have been wounded; sometimes that they have no other means of support" (232). The rest of the essay elaborates the idea that serious artists should consider adding such comments to their work: "I should like to see a Cubist putting down in crimson on the left-hand corner of his canvas, 'The best I can do'" (232). Or an artist who paints portraits of the wealthy could start to advertise: "Mr. Phillip Cobble, has painted two Duchesses and one Shareshuffler. He can also do animals, and he makes the dogs look like human beings" (233). Behind these jokes is Belloc's implication that the society artists are in fact no more adept than the pavement artist, who at least tries "to represent the thing which he pictures." But the essay is not a serious satire of art, merely a funny idea fleshed out.

"The Creative Muse" is based on the same principle: an examination of what would happen if everyone lied for no reason at all, what Belloc calls "gratuitous, cheerful and complete mendacity." This idea, like the one about artists, is only as funny as the writer makes it. Belloc knew that the best way to enliven the idea is to develop it, as in the following example:

> For instance, you go into a country inn near a railway station and you say, "Can you tell me when the next train goes to London?" The innkeeper answers, looking at his watch, "One of the best trains of the day has just gone, but if you care to take a short walk and come back at five minutes to six you will be in time to take the six two, which gets to Waterloo without stopping anywhere, except at Basingstoke. There is a 'third' Pullman on board and they serve a meal, if you want it." (279)

The traveler returns at 5:55 only to find that he missed the 5:45, and that the next train leaves around midnight. The humor in this passage derives from the elaborateness of the innkeeper's lie. If he had said simply, "The next train is the six two," the lie would have seemed only mean-spirited. By adding all of the helpful advice—about the specific times, the route, and the facilities—Belloc's innkeeper becomes not a simple liar, but a folk artist. After describing a few more of these lies—such as a man's telling his friend that it is "well worth going into town to see the charred remains of the Albert Hall," which burned down late last night—Belloc concludes with "a true story." He was on a large liner, waiting patiently as its scheduled departure time slipped by. After asking "a selection of officials" about the cause and extent of the delay and receiving widely differing answers, he met one young sailor who patiently explained the whole problem in great detail. "Naturally I did not believe a word he said; and he alone, as it turned out, had told me the truth and the exact truth in every detail. The moral of this, as of everything else, is that you never can tell" (285). The final laugh, appropriately enough, is at the reader's expense. But why should anyone expect an essay on the art of lying to be true?

## The Historical Essays

In "On Writing as a Trade," included in the collection *A Conversation with a Cat* (1931), Belloc laments the fact that writers are paid according to the length of what they produce: "Who would judge the value of a picture by its acreage?" (179) Belloc had to lengthen a number of his histories because of the desires of his publishers; several of the books would not have been written at all had he not owed his publishers money. In his historical essays, however, Belloc was free of the booksellers' restrictions.

*A Conversation with a Cat* includes a number of historical essays that demonstrate the various ways Belloc exploited this freedom. He was able to excerpt small dramatic scenes that did not need a broader context, discuss people or events that would not fit easily into larger studies, and convey images evoked by his visits to important historical sites.

"Laud on the Scaffold" exemplifies the dramatic historical scene that does not require an elaborate background. Although Laud was the Archbishop of Canterbury who was condemned to death because of his support for the doomed Charles I, Belloc begins his essay with only an elliptical reference to the circumstances: "It was Friday the 10th of January of the year 1645, and in the morning of the winter day, before it was light, that William Laud woke from a deep and quiet sleep, which had refreshed him, though he knew it to be the last sleep of his life" (117). It could be argued that many of Belloc's readers knew who Laud was and why he was to be executed, yet the unadorned reference to "William Laud" establishes the simple truth that sets the tone for the essay: a man was to be beheaded because of the beliefs he openly proclaimed.

The essay subtly contrasts the political and personal aspects of the execution. In describing Laud's self-defense before Parliament, for example, Belloc writes: "Such of the Commons as still remained had voted for death by an ordinance; and, of a score of such of the Lords as still remained, half a dozen may have voted the death of the old man. And indeed his blood had been promised to the Scotch" (118). The casual syntax of that final sentence economically conveys Belloc's point that Laud, the head of the Church of England, was to die because the political exigencies of the time demanded it. The collision of the personal and political appears again in Belloc's rendering of Laud's final moments on the scaffold: "He knelt, and in one more short prayer still used the twisted language of his time, and its metaphor: but in the midst of this he again enshrined a clear phrase among the rest—a prayer for England" (121). The drama of the execution itself followed—with the executioner holding the head up to the crowd—but the fact that Laud's final prayer was for England stays in the reader's mind. The economy imposed by the essay format becomes in Belloc's best historical sketches a means of dramatizing an immediate event and suggesting its greater implications.

The essay on "Charles Brandon, Duke of Suffolk" is totally devoid of drama and implications. A Renaissance courtier, husband of Henry VIII's sister Mary, Brandon was "all of one piece, as simple, as ridiculous, as despicable and as entrancing as any adventurer that ever stepped" (83). Brandon's story would never be a major part of a full-length study—he was too insignificant—but Belloc found him intriguing and therefore devoted a brief essay to him.

The first paragraph makes it clear that Belloc's interest in Brandon is nothing more than intense curiosity: "There is a whole procession of men, long dead, whom I should like to have met. But of late weeks during my reading I have been filled with a desire to have met Charles Brandon, Duke of Suffolk, more than any" (83). Belloc was fascinated, on a personal level, by a shining example of pure amorality: "When a man is as careless of honour and all the major and minor morals as that, when he goes prancing through life like a two-year-old and keeping it up to sixty, tell me, do you not agree with me? Is it not delightful?" (83) As in "Laud on the Scaffold," Belloc's tone is perfectly appropriate to his subject.

The essay "La Rochelle" represents another way in which Belloc's historical research provided the raw material for a brief discussion. La Rochelle is a small French coastal town that the Huguenots—the French Protestants—were defending against the forces of Cardinal Richelieu, the ruler during the reign of Louis XIII. Buckingham, a favorite of Charles I of England, tried unsuccessfully to relieve the besieged town and in the process lost thousands of soldiers. A separate essay on Buckingham is included in the collection, but "La Rochelle" is a record of Belloc's thoughts upon visiting the site, probably while researching *Richelieu.*

In studying La Rochelle, Belloc was struck by the way the town has remained frozen in time: "it has been fixed as by a spell just at that moment in its history when it was most famous, just at that moment after which its importance to European society disappeared" (153). Ironically, La Rochelle has been protected by the spirit of modern progress which has developed a neighboring town, La Pallice: "There you may see the great docks for the submarines, and the repairing sheds, and the warehouses, springing up; and the big new sea wall, and the great sandy spaces allotted and rapidly filling with buildings" (157). La Pallice will act as "a screen" or "a lightning conductor" for La Rochelle. The ancient city, which almost saw the English gain a foothold on the French coast, remains unchanged. "The mournful empty horizons are the same, and the sea birds complaining" (157). The fact that La Rochelle was preserved because of its proximity to a developing town has nothing to do with what made it famous, but in his essay Belloc makes this tiny bit of history come alive.

Belloc's full-length histories were repeatedly criticized for biases and willful distortions. In his essays, however, he was not battling the Whig historians but merely conveying scenes and images that struck him as interesting. On this small scale he was best able to exercise his great historical sensitivity and his gift of language.

Of all of his different kinds of writing, Belloc's essays received the most consistently enthusiastic reviews. Although an occasional commentator suggested that a collection contained less than meets the eye, most of the reviewers evaluated the books as what they were: volumes to be taken along on the train. Most of the critics enumerated defects in the essays and then surrendered to Belloc. The review of *Short Talks with the Dead* in the *Times Literary Supplement* is representative:

We have him here at his slightest, often in his least reasonable frame of mind, sometimes frankly clowning and not always giving us his best clowning; and yet almost every one of these short papers leaves an impression of wit and strength and the soundest of prose. There is hardly another writer of today who could impart to random musings of this sort a pungency like the tang of bitter ale—pre-war, let us hasten to add.[9]

The essay was a successful medium for Belloc because of his mastery of English prose. Percy Hutchison, writing of *A Conversation with a Cat* in the *New York Times*, isolated the appeal of the essays:

One does not read far in this book . . . without reaching the opinion that there is one word that applies above all others—the much abused word "style." In every best sense of the term every page glows with that soft, irridescent light that can come from language only when used by one who loves language for its own sake, one who is sensitive to the fine flower of expression. . . . It is for his style that Hilaire Belloc will be read when many a volume more weighty has passed into obscurity.[10]

Hutchison was right: most of the essays are enjoyable reading today because no matter what he talked about, Belloc was a great talker.

## Chapter Six
# The Works of Controversy

The English reading public would have been surprised indeed to learn that Hilaire Belloc wished to be remembered as a poet, for he had earned his considerable reputation primarily as a commentator on current events. During World War I, for instance, his weekly analyses of the European fighting were widely read. When his government was not at war, Belloc was a relentless critic of the political, economic, and religious ruling class. In a torrent of poems, articles, pamphlets, and novels he employed his talents for ridicule, parody, satire, and logical argumentation in a frontal assault on the English establishment. Four of Belloc's public controversies concerned vitally important issues of the day.

The first controversy was created by his publication in 1911 of *The Party System*, which argued that the political structure of contemporary England was wholly unrepresentative, that Parliament was controlled by the powerful leaders of the two parties who were interested only in perpetuating their own power. In *The House of Commons and Monarchy* (1920), Belloc proposed a return to some form of monarchy as a means of protecting the weak citizens from the powerful.

The second controversy concerned Belloc's argument that England was not only politically unfree, but economically unfree as well. *The Servile State* (1912) was his prophetic warning that the nation was quickly losing its spirit of economic independence by drifting toward a state in which the average citizen would be forced to work for a wealthy industrialist because all of the means of production would be concentrated in a few hands. *An Essay on the Restoration of Property* (1936) was a statement of Belloc's strategy for restoring the means of production to the people.

The third, and most violent, controversy followed the publication of *The Jews* (1922), an analysis of the growing tension between the Jews and non-Jews in England and Europe. Belloc felt that the Jews as a group exercised disproportionate influence, especially in international finance. Arguing that the Jews are a separate race from Europeans, he advocated a policy of segregation within the various European nations as a means of lessening the tensions. His prophecies that tensions would eventually lead to widespread persecution of the Jews were soon confirmed by the Nazis.

The publication of H. G. Wells's *Outline of History* (1920) led to the fourth public battle of Belloc's life. Responding to a work that he felt had insulted his church, he began a feud with Wells that lasted more than a year and produced three different polemical volumes, two of them by Belloc. With the bulk of contemporary scientific opinion supporting him, he undercut Wells's espousal of Darwinism. In pressing his attack further and turning it into a sweeping defense of Catholicism, he succeeded only in undermining his own credibility.

## Belloc on Politics

When Hilaire Belloc wrote about the Jews, about economics, and about science, he was writing as an informed amateur. When he turned his attention to the political structure, as he did in *The Party System*, he was approaching his subject as an insider. The years he had spent as a member of Parliament were probably the most disappointing and difficult time in his entire professional life. Belloc refused to stand for reelection in 1910 because he felt increasingly frustrated by what he saw as the ineffectuality and corruption of English government. Before resigning from Parliament, he castigated his colleagues for participating in a meaningless charade of party loyalties. He argued that the distinction between the government and the opposition party was a sham, that the parties no longer stood for clear policies. In a later speech to some local constituents he declared that he was glad to have left "the dirtiest company it has ever been my misfortune to keep."[1]

*The Party System* (1911), which he wrote in collaboration with Cecil Chesterton, is Belloc's formal indictment of Parliament. The purpose of the book is announced in the Preface: "to destroy and to supplant the system under which Parliament . . . has been rendered null" (8). The general thesis of *The Party System* is that the government of Great Britain was representative only in name. The adversary relationship between the two major political parties no longer existed. In its place was an unspoken alliance between the leaders of the two parties that enabled them to maintain the powers and perquisites of office while thwarting any constructive reform initiated by the lesser members of Parliament.

According to Belloc and Chesterton, admission to the magic circle of insiders was restricted to relatives or to the rich. After identifying the intricate web of family relationships that linked the chief rulers of the two parties, the authors suggest the implications of this situation:

We are not surprised at Romeo loving Juliet, though he is a Montague and she a Capulet. But if we found in addition that Lady Capulet was by birth a Montague, that Lady Montague was the first cousin of Old Capulet, that Mercutio was at once the nephew of a Capulet and the brother-in-law of a Montague, that County Paris was related on his father's side to one house and on his mother's side to the other, that Tybalt was Romeo's uncle's stepson, and that the Friar who married Romeo and Juliet was Juliet's uncle and Romeo's first cousin once removed, we should probably conclude that the feud between the two houses was being kept up mainly for the dramatic entertainment of the people of Verona. (41–42)

This concentration of power in the hands of the party elders affected every aspect of parliamentary life. The party leaders controlled the debate by allotting little time for matters they wanted to ignore or by simply burying them through legislative maneuvering. And because the party leaders controlled the secret campaign funds, upstarts and outsiders could be effectively eliminated from Parliament.

After defining the problem as they saw it, Belloc and Chesterton turn to the question of reforming Parliament, but unfortunately their proposals are thin. They advocate two main measures: first, holding regular parliamentary elections, such as every four years, and making the government indissoluble between elections; and second, substituting for the system of ministers a structure of departmental committees, which the ministers could chair, but not control. Involving the back benchers more directly in the framing of legislation, Belloc and Chesterton predicted, would decentralize power.

Underlying both of these reforms, however, is the need for an educated and active electorate:

. . . changes in political machinery will prove either impossible or ineffective, unless the people can be awakened to political consciousness and to a resolution to make their will prevail. An alert democracy, even with unchanged machinery, could knock the bottom out of the Party System to-morrow by refusing to elect party hacks and by sending to Parliament men fully determined to make an end of the corruption and unreality of our politics. In proportion as the mass of men understand the nature of the present system, and resolve to replace it by a better, the Party System will become more and more difficult to work. (193–94)

Belloc and Chesterton's concept of how to publicize new ideas creates the major flaw of *The Party System*. "The truth," they write, "when it is spoken for some useful purpose, must necessarily seem obscure, extravagant, or merely false; for, were it of common knowledge, it would not be worth expressing." Rather than using a restrained and understated style, buttressing their assertions with carefully documented facts, the authors often lapse into overstatement. For example, Parliament "affords today . . . no more than an opportunity for highly lucrative careers . . . founded upon the bamboozlement of the public . . . with the complicity of nobodies content to write M. P. after their name . . ." (185). Or, in another passage, "The necessity of being rid of . . . [the Party System] . . . is like the necessity . . . of being rid of a great dead body in one's neighbourhood when it has begun to putrefy" (157).

As Harold Cox wrote in the *Saturday Review*, the book "is well worth reading, even though the perusal will bring a good deal of disappointment. For the authors have made the profound blunder of overstating their case."[2]

Nine years after *The Party System*, Belloc published *The House of Commons and Monarchy* (1920), which is in effect its sequel. The thesis of the later book is that the only alternative to the decayed House of Commons is monarchy. By monarchy Belloc means "any man or woman or child, but normally an adult man . . . who is responsible ultimately to the commonwealth for the general conduct and preservation of the commonwealth at any one moment" (173–74). Although he grants that history affords numerous examples of monarchs who have misused their powers, Belloc maintains that endowing in one person the central power of government is the only means of protecting the weak from the strong and of maintaining the power of the state as a whole. As an example of an effective monarchy, he suggests the institution of the presidency in the United States. On how such a centralized power might evolve in England, however, he offers no specifics.

*The House of Commons and Monarchy* was received with little enthusiasm. The *Times Literary Supplement* review was representative: "Mr. Belloc has written a vivacious and suggestive essay, which has the merit of returning to first principles, but which yet leaves the feeling that his treatment is too slight."[3] The public had been willing to grant Belloc a certain authority in his 1911 indictment of Parliament, but it saw no reason to pay much attention to his vague and inconclusive proposals in 1920. He had become irrelevant as a political theorist. In the next decade the rise of fascism in Europe made his proposals for the strengthening of the central authority repugnant.

## Belloc on Economics

Belloc's thinking about contemporary economics was as unorthodox as his thinking about religion, politics, literature, or most other aspects of current life. Whereas the English state was moving swiftly toward socialism, the so-called welfare state that still exists, Belloc preached the virtues of an economic system called distributism.[4]

Distributism, as Belloc defines it in *The Servile State* (1912),[5] is an economic system by which "the mass of citizens should severally own the means of production"(6). The other three alternative economic systems he defines as capitalism, in "which the few free citizens control the means of production while the rest have not such property" (15); collectivism (socialism), "the placing of the means of production in the hands of the political officers of the community" (5); and the servile state, "in which those who do not own the means of production shall be legally compelled to work for those who do, and shall receive in exchange a security of livelihood" (6). Belloc's central idea is that while England was consciously attempting to transform its unstable form of capitalism—a transitory phase—into socialism, it was creating in fact the servile state.

Belloc was impelled to write down his argument following his public debate with Ramsay MacDonald.[6] While MacDonald's defense of socialism was practical, Belloc's plea for distributism was based on abstract reasoning, history, and even religion. The debate, like most of Belloc's public performances, was an exciting theatrical event, but it was not a closely reasoned intellectual confrontation. *The Servile State* was his attempt to articulate his case clearly.

The first sentence of the book is characteristic of Belloc's expository prose in its straightforward self-confidence:

This book is written to maintain and prove the following truth:—

That our free modern society in which the means of production are owned by a few being necessarily in unstable equilibrium, it is tending to reach a condition of stable equilibrium BY THE ESTABLISHMENT OF COMPULSORY LABOUR LEGALLY ENFORCIBLE UPON THOSE WHO DO NOT OWN THE MEANS OF PRODUCTION FOR THE ADVANTAGE OF THOSE WHO DO. (3)

This servile state would consist of two classes of citizens: those who were politically and economically free, and those "economically unfree and politically unfree, but at first secured by their very lack of freedom in certain necessaries of life and in a minimum of well-being beneath which they shall not fall" (3).

Oddly enough, Belloc tries to make the book seem a description of the servile state, and not an evaluation of it. In the Preface to the second edition he goes out of his way to disclaim any motives beyond simple exposition: "I say nowhere in the book that the reestablishment of slavery would be a bad thing as compared with our present insecurity, and no one has a right to read such an opinion into this book."[7] But his constant use of the term "slavery" as a synonym for "servile state" is only one of the more obvious clues that the book is, like almost everything else he wrote, a moral argument.

Typical Belloc arguments emerge when he presents his historical analysis of economics in the western world. The pagan world relied extensively on the institution of slavery, but medieval Europe, with its serfs, freeholders, and guilds, saw the flowering of the distributist state. Men owned the land they tilled and were economically independent and secure. What was at the root of this "excellent consummation of human society"? Belloc answers this question only elliptically when he defines the marvelous "transformation which had come over European society in the course of ten Christian centuries" (51). But this Edenic interlude was not to last; the "dreadful moral anarchy" (52) of capitalism was set in motion by the weakness and lust of Henry VIII. As Belloc argues again and again in his histories and biographies, Henry's split with the Catholic Church over the issue of his divorce from Catherine of Aragon led to the confiscation of the monastic lands and wealth, a process which in turn led to the establishment of a wealthy gentry that instituted the capitalistic economic structure. By bringing the argument back to his insistent thesis—the tragedy of the English Reformation—he effectively if not intentionally clarifies the purpose of *The Servile State*.

The fact that Belloc was invoking his favorite subject surprised no one. All the public figures who took on Belloc—MacDonald, H. G. Wells, Bernard Shaw—obviously knew what argument they were going to get from the Catholic apologist, but his extraordinary breadth of learning and rhetorical skill made him a powerful adversary. The criticism of *The Servile State* was not that Belloc was wrong in seeing England moving toward a condition of economic servitude, but that he provided no clear proposals for how to achieve the distribution of property among the citizens in a modern industrial state.

Belloc was quite aware that he offered no practical plan for distribution (109). In fact, he provides several reasons that would indeed make a distributist state almost impossible to achieve: the enormous bureaucratic difficulties involved in dividing up a large and complex piece of property, the inability of small property owners to raise the capital necessary for productive growth, and, most important, the fact that the public no longer think of themselves as property owners: "Is not the whole psychology of a Capitalist society divided between the proletarian mass which thinks in terms not of property but of 'employment,' and the few owners who are alone familiar with the machinery of administration?" (111) Belloc concludes his prophetic tract by expressing his hope "that the Faith will recover its intimate and guiding place in the heart of Europe" (189) and thereby reverse the trend toward economic slavery. His discussion of how to create a distributist state did not appear until twenty-four years later.

In 1936 Belloc published *An Essay on the Restoration of Property*.[8] In 1912 *The Servile State* sounded reactionary; in 1936, with the world economy in chaos from the great depression and with the rise of Nazism in Europe, his discussion of ways to encourage the "peasantry" sounded perversely eccentric. But he had no illusions that the task would be easy. As he writes in the Preface to *An Essay*, reversing modern trends "is not *quite* impossible . . . at least, it is not quite impossible to start the beginnings of a change" (12).

Belloc suggests no detailed plan; the restoration of property "must essentially be the product of a new mood, not of a new scheme. It must grow from seed planted in the breast" (11). He saw his opponents as so formidable that nothing could be accomplished by a direct assault. Picturing himself as a man with garden shears trying to cut down a tree, he declares that his tools are too feeble for injuring the trunk or uprooting the tree, too feeble for destroying the branches, *"but not too feeble for clipping leaves"* (66).

The measures he recommended in the book were in fact quite a bit more radical than his metaphor would suggest. His two major proposals were to restore the small craftsman and farmer by means of a graduated taxation that would penalize growth beyond a certain limit, and to divide up the ownership of enterprises such as railroads that must of necessity remain large. Although he realized that the expense of supporting a modern industrial state requires heavy taxation, and that heavy taxation requires a substantial body of wealthy owners who can be taxed at a high rate, he argued that the possibility of economic freedom justifies the hardship of a distributist state.

Belloc knew that a man cannot make a chair as cheaply as a factory can. When you purchase a "well-made piece of furniture, neither repulsive nor mechanical in design . . . you are buying something for society at that price . . . that 'something' is citizenship, and the escape from slavery" (77–78). As it has turned out, citizens in the modern industrial world have defined economic freedom differently from Belloc. Whereas he thought of freedom as a function of production, modern workers think of it as a function of consumption. He advocated small, independent producers whereas workers today are less interested in how goods and services are provided and more interested in how to protect their ability to purchase them. Belloc probably would have had trouble accepting the notion that economic freedom can be thought of as the ability to purchase furniture made of plastic or cardboard—or of hand-carved mahogany.

## Belloc on the Jews

That Hilaire Belloc was a Catholic apologist was known by everyone who followed English letters; that he was an anti-Semite was almost as widely believed. The charge surfaced everywhere, even in the unlikeliest contexts. Of Belloc's *Milton*, for example, the literary critic E. M. W. Tillyard wrote sarcastically, "It would have been still more delightful if Milton had been a Jew and Mr. Belloc had not been constrained, by the apparently serious form he chose, to preserve the semblance of moderation."[9] Even today the charge is stated almost casually, as if it were an incontrovertible fact and as if "anti-Semitism" has a single, clear meaning.[10]

The source of the public impression that Belloc was anti-Semitic was probably his early political novels, several of which present the villainous Jewish businessman I. Z. Barnett. Belloc clearly defines Barnett as an unscrupulous usurer and manipulator who wants money and power and cares nothing about whom he destroys in achieving his goals. In addition to these novels, *The Mercy of Allah* was published with a dust jacket that identified the amoral and hypocritical protagonist as a Jewish millionaire. This was done by the publisher, without Belloc's knowledge.[11]

The book that crystallized the public perception of Belloc as an anti-Semite, however, was *The Jews* (1922), which offers an analysis of "the Jewish problem." Belloc was fully aware that the book would be controversial, for a Jewish advisor to whom he submitted the text before it was published told him that the book was unjust and that Jews would neither read it nor sell it.[12] Still, Belloc had no idea of the extent to which the general public would misinterpret what he meant to say.

The goal of *The Jews*, as Belloc states it in the Preface, was to reduce the distrust and fear that exist between the Jews and non-Jews. "I have written it as an attempt at justice" (ix). [13] Belloc hoped that, by raising a question society would rather ignore, he could initiate an open and constructive dialogue.

The first sentence of the book announces his thesis:

...that the continued presence of the Jewish nation intermixed with other nations alien to it presents a permanent problem of the gravest character: that the wholly different culture, tradition, race and religion of Europe make Europe a permanent antagonist to Israel, and that the recent and rapid intensification of that antagonism gives to the discovery of a solution immediate and highly practical importance. (3)

Belloc's contention that Jews are a race separate from Europeans is the basis of his argument. He states that as a separate race, and not just a people of a different faith, the Jews have never been absorbed into the European culture, despite their talent for "superficial mutation"— the ability to seem German in Germany, French in France.

Belloc sees four causes of the friction between the Jews and non-Jews. He accuses the Jews of two: an open sense of superiority to the Europeans and a secrecy about being Jewish, as exemplified by their practice of changing their names. The Europeans he accuses of the other two causes of friction: "a persistent disingenuousness in our treatment of this minority" and "unintelligence in their treatment" (140). Although he claims not to be proposing a solution to the problem, he states that the tension could be reduced if each side ceased acting in those ways that are obnoxious to the other. On the question of a homeland he argues that the British protectorate in Palestine for the Jews would prove a constant irritant to the neighboring Arabs. The solution, he felt, lay in Jewish self-government, within the various European countries or Palestine, but his discussion of this proposal is very brief.

Despite Belloc's attempts in *The Jews* to be objective—by balancing his criticism of both groups—his whole method of analysis lent itself to a misinterpretation of his intended point. Whether or not the readers agreed with him that the Jews constitute a separate race, the book leaves no question that he saw Jews as separate and distinct from Europeans. A noisy and foolish passage such as the following is characteristic of Belloc's style at its least attractive:

When you meet a Jew, whether you are his enemy or his friend, you meet a Jew. He has a certain expression, a certain manner, certain physical characteristics which you may not be able to analyse at the moment you see him, but which give you the impression and the certitude that you are dealing with a particular thing, to wit, the Jewish race. (297—98)

The tone of this passage certainly suggests derision, but Belloc would maintain that he meant only what he literally said. In his defense, it is true that in everything he did he classified and enumerated. In discussing another book about the Jewish question, for instance, he asserted that the major flaw was that the author believed assimilation to be possible, which would be as impossible as "to make the English shallow and cynical, the French unmilitary or the Germans delicate and the Irish orderly."[14]

The charges of anti-Semitism hurt Belloc deeply. In the Preface to the 1928 second edition of *The Jews*, he defends himself, explaining that his fictional satires are directed only against Jewish financiers, and in no way imply "a general attitude toward the Jewish people" (xvi).

Of more interest than Belloc's perfunctory denial of the charge of anti-Semitism—he even points out that he has many Jewish friends— is a curious passage in the Preface to the second edition. In qualifying his thesis that the Jews are wholly separate from the culture of Europe, he provides this comment: "There are the strongest examples, which any one of us with a sufficient knowledge of Europe can call to mind and reverently praise, of Jews and Jewesses who have deliberately attached themselves to the Christian culture and especially to the Catholic Church, having discovered Her to be Divine" (xiii). And at the end of the Preface appears another revealing passage: "There is an old prophecy, perhaps no more than a superstition, but arresting, that in the end they [the Jews] will accept the consummation of the mystery of which they were the first and immemorial custodians; that is, that they will accept the Faith" (xvii). Whereas Belloc disliked certain characteristics he saw in Jews, it is likely that his central quarrel with them was that they were not Catholic. Like Moslems or Buddhists, they were separate and different from him, and so he defined them, bluntly and often indelicately.

Apart from providing some insight to its author, *The Jews* is a chillingly prophetic work in its analysis of the probable results of the tension between the Jews and non-Jews. In discussing the general antagonism to powerful Jews in finance, Belloc predicts that the relationship "will probably cease in violence. The danger is that if it ceases in violence a vast number of innocent will be involved with the guilty" (96).

In a new first chapter included in the third edition (1937) he describes the first stages of Nazi persecution of the Jews as "racial vanity gone mad" (xlv). Although Belloc could not foresee the catastrophe of the Holocaust, he knew the Nazis would ultimately be destroyed: "Israel is eternal, and Nazidom most certainly not eternal" (xliii).

*The Jews* excited more intense critical reaction than any other of his books. While some commentators saw the book as noble, wise, and constructive and many saw it as well-meaning but flawed by factual inaccuracies, a number of readers were so incensed by the book that they lost all of their objectivity. The usually reliable *New York Times*, for instance, printed a long review that included comments such as this: "no one would take . . . [Belloc] . . . for a friend of the Jew, or of humanity, or, indeed of anything normally associated with the concerns of modern civilization." Later in the review, the writer even implied that Belloc was a coward for only writing about the recent war, without being in the fighting. [15] In fact, despite his age—forty-four—Belloc offered his services to his government on several occasions and was disappointed that it could find no official place for him. [16] Only after the refusal did he turn to war journalism.

A more responsible review appeared in the *Times Literary Supplement* which praised Belloc's attempts at objectivity but criticized his unexamined contention that Jews are a separate race: "It is the racial characteristics with which he is always concerned, but he never pauses to consider how far these characteristics are due to the religious tie. But this is really fundamental to the whole problem." [17]

The best discussion of Belloc and anti-Semitism is by David Lodge, who isolated two causes of Belloc's attitude toward the Jews: the vague myth, perpetuated for centuries and not rejected by the Vatican until decades after his death, that Jews were responsible for the crucifixion; and the association of Jews with usury and therefore with industrial capitalism. Lodge's conclusion is reasonable: ". . . though both men [Belloc and G. K. Chesterton] were too humane and too intelligent to indulge in the hateful and irrational kind of anti-Semitism which prepared the way for Hitler's policy of genocide, they often seem to be either unconsciously or irresponsibly flirting with it."[18]

Belloc recognized the growing tensions caused by the Jewish presence in Europe and had the courage to confront the problem directly and soberly, but his temperament and rhetorical style rendered him wholly incapable of achieving his goal: to lessen the tensions. All that he achieved was a reputation as an anti-Semite.

## The Feud with H. G. Wells

Of all of Belloc's many public controversies, the most bitter and personal feud was waged with H. G. Wells, the extraordinarily popular novelist who is best remembered today for his science fiction. The feud began in 1920 when Wells started publishing his massive *Outline of History* in installments. Wells's history of mankind was written from a "progressive," "scientific" point of view, which Belloc could not abide. Consequently, he wrote a series of twenty-four articles attacking Wells's book and published them in three different Catholic periodicals. Wells then wrote six articles in rebuttal, but the journals refused them, even when he offered them without charge. Rather than accepting one of the journals' offer of the "opportunity of correcting definite points of fact upon which he might have been misrepresented," Wells published his articles in book form, *Mr. Belloc Objects to "The Outline of History"* (1926). Belloc responded almost immediately with *Mr. Belloc Still Objects to Mr. Wells's "Outline of History"* (1926). Unwilling to let that be his last word, Belloc revised his original twenty-four articles into a book, *A Companion to Mr. Wells's "Outline of History"* (1926).

Although Belloc and Wells argued about many of the ideas in the *Outline of History*, one central idea was the basis of the entire feud: Wells's defense of Darwinism. In explaining evolution, Wells was an orthodox Darwinian, citing natural selection as the most plausible explanation for the birth and death of species. Those characteristics that help an organism survive in its environment are perpetuated because the fittest survive and reproduce whereas the less fit perish. In this way the species evolve over the course of countless generations.

Belloc accepted the concept of natural selection, which he considered merely common sense: animals that can run fast will tend to live longer because they can capture more prey and evade more predators. What he did not accept was the idea that natural selection *caused* evolution: "The theory of Natural Selection as the *agent* of Evolution does not mean that floods drown cattle and don't drown fish. We all know that. The theory means that successive floods turn cattle into fish—and that is a very different proposition!" (18) Wells believed that all species are always in a state of transition, responding to the changes in their environments; Belloc believed in fixed forms: a pig is a pig, a dog is a dog, and a man is a man.

How, then, did Belloc account for new species, if they did not evolve out of existing ones? The answer, for him, was simple: new species were created by Design, that is, by God. This, then, was the crux of the Belloc-Wells feud: "the essential quarrel . . . between those for whom the Universe is blind and those who see it to be the work of God" (12).

Ironically, Belloc had the weight of scientific opinion behind him when he attacked Darwinism. In the early decades of the century Darwinism lost favor in the scientific community, not because it contradicted the theological perspective espoused by Belloc and others, but because it failed to explain the origin of those characteristics that enabled the "fittest" to survive. Subsequent research in genetics has provided the information that has ultimately vindicated Darwin's basic theory, but in 1926 Belloc in fact humiliated Wells. Never merciful when he discovered his antagonist's flaw, he skillfully documented the prevailing scientific opinion that supported his assault on Darwinism.

Belloc undermined his own argument, however, by refusing to restrict himself to an indictment of Wells's science. By broadening his scope to include the theological question, he sacrificed his objectivity. The first sentence of his *Companion*, for instance, reads, "My object in these pages is to follow, for Catholic readers, Mr. Wells's *Outline of History* . . ." (1). Other comments scattered throughout

Belloc's attack make it clear that his object was to provide a forum for his own beliefs, not for a measured examination of the issues:

. . . *all* Catholics . . . affirm . . . [the doctrine of Original Sin] . . . because, whether pleasant or unpleasant, it is true. (32)

. . . sympathy or antagonism with the Catholic Faith is the only thing of real importance in attempting to teach History . . . (47)

Belloc's whole motive, as he states near the end of his *Companion*, was "to examine whether Mr. Wells were competent as an historian to attack the Faith of Christian men . . ." (103).

The critical response to the protracted feud between Belloc and Wells was a mixture of fascination and embarrassment. Darwinism and its implications for traditional religious interpretations of the nature of reality were popular topics, and a number of commentators discussed which contestant "won" the debate. P. W. Wilson, writing in the *New York Times*, is representative in his assessment of the debate on fixed forms: "While . . . Mr. Wells may have the truth on his side, it is Mr. Belloc who can produce the more immediate evidence."[19] Many commentators, however, were more interested in the tone of the debate between the pugnacious Catholic and the sophisticated free-thinker. In his rebuttal, *Mr. Belloc Objects*, Wells characterizes Belloc's original attacks as "grossly personal and provocative in tone" (v). Clearly, Wells did not enjoy the personal aspect of the feud, and most critics agreed that "Mr. Belloc is a very able controversialist while Mr. Wells is temperamentally incapable of effective argumentation."[20] Perhaps the most satisfying comment is that "the whole controversy is becoming unbearable . . . they should lock themselves in a chapel or a laboratory and not disturb the public. Both writers have been guilty of language that is more violent than their arguments are clear."[21] Belloc was oblivious to this kind of comment, for he had achieved his object: he had given comfort to his fellow Catholics by humiliating an enemy of their religion.

The quarrel with H. G. Wells reveals Belloc's polemical style. He was never modulated, restrained, and understated. When he chose an enemy, he fought completely, with all of the weapons he could find.

Until the enemy was not only disarmed but conquered, Belloc pressed the attack. As one commentator put it, "He hurls his facts into the fray like so many jagged stones."[22] H. G. Wells was certainly not alone in calling Belloc's polemical style personal and provocative.

What Belloc never learned was that his style was largely ineffective in the service of an unusual and unpopular idea: he believed that people listened only if his voice was shrill and his argument sweeping and simple. When the English public ignored his criticism, he raised his voice, but the louder he talked, the less they listened. Eventually, the frenzy of his arguments all but completely discredited him as a serious analyst of the current scene. Except for his partisan Catholic audience, the general reading public began to believe that he was arguing because he loved to argue, not because he believed passionately in an idea.

Behind all of his works of controversy, however, lay the same idea that motivated the bulk of his writings. He desired above all else to re-create in twentieth-century England the Europe of the Middle Ages. He longed for the world in which peasants owned the land they worked, raised their families in peace, and prayed to God. He wanted to return to the pre-Reformation England of a strong monarch and a united church, before the wealthy ruling class had stolen the monastic properties, subverted the king, and created a ruthless capitalist economy that enriched the powerful at the cost of the average citizen's freedom.

Of course, Belloc never seriously expected to accomplish this. What he did expect, however, was that his ideas would create a substantial intellectual debate that would slow down what he considered to be England and Europe's decline. But his temperament, turn of mind, and polemical style prevented, to a large degree, even this. Viewed across the gulf of more than half a century, his major works of controversy record his unsuccessful attempts to restructure a world he saw as unjust. Belloc was never content with compromises, and he at least had the satisfaction of knowing that he could not be accused of trying to make peace with that unjust world.

# Chapter Seven
# The Travel Books

During the middle three decades of his life, Belloc spent relatively little time at his home in Sussex. As early as 1895 he became an itinerant teacher, working for the extension divisions of Oxford and London University. In addition to these academic lectures, he spoke on numerous subjects across the whole of Great Britain and the United States. His influential war journalism boosted his popularity as a lecturer; even as late as the 1920s, he was away from home nearly every week. When Belloc was not on a lecture tour, he was likely to be almost anywhere in England or Europe, preparing for his current historical study or biography. In researching the Napoleonic campaigns, for instance, he traveled from France through Germany and Poland to Moscow.

Even when his trips were unrelated to his work, Belloc tried to write something about the area, for he knew that one way or another he would be able to sell anything he produced. *Many Cities* (1928) and *Places* (1942) are collections of essays linked by their common theme. *The Contrast* (1923), a comparison of the United States and England, was written after Belloc completed a lecture tour of America. And when he was convalescing in Algeria from a near-fatal case of pneumonia, he wrote *Esto Perpetua* (1906) about the history and geography of North Africa.

Belloc was interested not only in places, but also in the physical network that connected them. *The Road* (1923) and *The Highway and its Vehicles* (1926) are technical studies, and *The Old Road* (1904), *The Historic Thames* (1907), and *The Pyrenees* (1909) are historical studies.

Three of Belloc's travel books—*The Path to Rome* (1902), *The Four Men* (1912), and *The Cruise of the "Nona"* (1925)—stand apart from the others in several ways. Structurally, each of the three is a combination of songs, anecdotes, and opinions, all held together, often rather tenuously, by Belloc's narrative about his trip. For example, he is perfectly happy in each of the three books to tell the reader that since nothing very interesting is happening to him at the moment, he will take this opportunity to analyze the recent decline of Parliament, or tell the story of the man who fooled the Devil. A few pages into one of these digressions he is likely to break off because he has just come upon an interesting inn or a curious person he would rather tell the reader about; he will get back to his digression some other time.

Belloc's refusal to stick to the travel narrative is not a structural gimmick; rather, it is the essence of these three books. He is certainly not writing about his destination. Nor is he primarily interested in providing a chronicle of the journey. The territory Belloc is describing in these books is his own sensibility. His focus is the interplay among his senses, his emotions, and his rational mind as he confronts the physical universe, the artifacts of man, and, of course, man himself. Taken together, these books constitute Belloc's spiritual autobiography.

### The Path to Rome

*The Path to Rome* (1902) is Belloc's record of a walking tour from Toul, France, to Rome in June, 1901. His motivation for making the trip is explained in the Preface: when revisiting his birthplace at La Celle St. Cloud one day, he went in'to pray at a church which had been renovated after his family had fled to Paris in 1870. Seeing a beautiful statue of the Virgin, he vowed "to go to Rome on Pilgrimage . . . I will walk all the way and take advantage of no wheeled thing . . . and I will be present at High Mass in St. Peter's on the Feast of St. Peter and St. Paul" (viii). Reginald Jebb, Belloc's son-in-law, speculated that the real motive for the pilgrimage was Belloc's feelings of guilt about his overwhelming commitment to politics, history, and his friends, about having to be brought back to an active faith in the church by his wife, Elodie. [1] As Belloc states simply in *The Path to Rome*, "It is a good thing to have loved one woman from a child, and it is a good thing not to have to return to the Faith" (161).

Once he decided to travel to Rome, why did he choose to do it on foot? First, he wanted to demonstrate the humility necessary for any religious pilgrimage. Second, he had no money. Elodie in fact had considerable trouble raising five pounds to forward to Milan to finance the last portion of her husband's trip. But even if they had had the money, he probably would have chosen to walk, for his other great pilgrimage, to propose to Elodie in San Francisco, was largely a walk across the western United States. And Belloc loved long-distance walking, even when the trip had no special symbolic meaning. As he explained in a letter years later:

One of the few wise things I have done . . . has been . . . to take those prodigious walks across the world: from the Pacific to the crest of the Sierras through Colorado, from Oxford to the Irish Sea, from York to Edinburgh, to Rome, from Toledo (slowly) to Toulouse, from the Basque country to Santiago: they do furnish the mind.[2]

As a long-distance walker, he was strong and fast: he held the Oxford undergraduate record of eleven and one-half hours for the walk from the university to London.[3]

In an introduction he wrote for *The Footpath Way: An Anthology for Walkers*[4] Belloc explains the appeal of walking: it is the natural form of human transportation. "A man walking becomes the cousin or the brother of everything round" (8). In a whimsical passage later in the introduction, he defines the metaphysics of walking: "What you really do, man, when you want to get to that distant place (and let this be a parable of all adventure and of all desire) is to take an enormous risk, the risk of coming down bang and breaking something: you lift one foot off the ground, and, as though that were not enough, you deliberately throw your centre of gravity forward so that you begin to fall" (4–5). Belloc walked to Rome because a man walking "sends his equilibrium to the devil . . . " and thus opens himself up to the possibility of spiritual growth (9).

To make his pilgrimage to Rome even more elemental, Belloc whenever possible avoided roads and railway tracks. In part, he wanted to stay away from what he called the "drawn, sad, jaded tourists" and the bawling and howling guides (223). Belloc's plan, however, was not merely to avoid the rich tourists, the spiritually unregenerate who follow the easy, sinful route. In fact, what he did was walk a straight line from Toul to Rome. While he encountered

obvious obstacles—rivers, forests, and even the Alps—it was fundamental to his conception of the pilgrimage: "only by following the
straight line" can one "pass from ridge to ridge and have this full
picture of the way he has been" (71). The subtle multiplicity of this
last phrase, in which "way" means both "route" and "essence,"
suggests the theme and power of *The Path to Rome*.

As a travelogue of Belloc's experiences on his march of almost four
hundred miles, the book is often exciting. At one point the straight
line draws him through a dark and gloomy forest. The shadows of the
leaves create a shifting pattern of night and twilight:

On every side the perspective of these bare innumerable shafts . . . merged
into recesses of distance where all light disappeared, yet . . . the slight
gloaming still surrounded me, as did the stillness framed in the drip of
water, and beneath my feet was the level carpet of the pine needles deadening
and making distant every tiny noise. (91−92)

In perhaps the greatest passage of natural description in the book,
Belloc recounts how he and a local guide attempted to cross over a pass
in the Alps and break through to Italy. After crawling across the ice
and snow for some time, they began to realize their danger: "the
wind was blowing a very full gale and roared past our ears. The surface
snow was whirring furiously like dust before it: past our faces and
against them drove the snow flakes, cutting the air: not falling, but
making straight darts and streaks. They seemed like the form of the
whistling wind; they blinded us" (244). Throughout the trip, Belloc
wore only the thin cotton suit he had purchased for a few shillings; his
boots had long since separated from their soles.

As powerful as many of the descriptive passages are, they are not
the core of *The Path to Rome*. Belloc declares his real subject: "My
pilgrimage is to Rome, my business is with lonely places, hills, and
the recollection of the spirit" (295). The central passage of the book is
his attempt to define his state of mind when he first saw the Alps:

Up there, the sky above and below them, part of the sky, but part of us, the
great peaks made communion between that homing creeping part of me
which loves vineyards and dances and a slow movement among pastures, and

that other part which is only properly at home in Heaven. . . . These, the great Alps, seen thus, link one in some way to one's immortality. . . . Let me put it thus: . . . I saw, as it were, my religion. (180)

On the flyleaf of the copy of *The Path to Rome* that he presented to his son-in-law, Belloc inscribed, "I wrote this book for the glory of God."[5]

For all of its essential seriousness, *The Path to Rome* is never solemn. In fact, it is probably Belloc's most high-spirited book, filled with youthful vitality and intoxicating charm. It begins with "Praise of This Book," in which he parodies conventional prefaces that catalog a group of unknown "nincompoops" and "say 'my thanks are due to such and such' all in a litany, as though any one cared a farthing for the rats!" (x) Belloc's preface proceeds to thank, among others, "the best authors of the Renaissance," Erasmus, the Nine Muses, the Three Graces, Bacchus, and Apollo. Another comic device, employed several times throughout the book, is a running debate between Auctor (the author) and Lector (the reader). Lector is a boring pedant who has his own ideas of what is properly part of a travel book: he would not discuss emotion or religion or tell stories. Above all, he would be terse. Auctor replies with a Rabelaisian tirade that concludes with these words: "There should be no verbosity in your style (God forbid!), still less pomposity, animosity, curiosity, or ferocity; . . . You would be led into no hilarity, charity, vulgarity, or barbarity" (415). The debate goes on. Belloc just wrote spontaneously—most of the book was written during the march—with no regard for the structure and content of a traditional travel book. He tells stories written in the newspapers in which his ham sandwich is wrapped. If he does not want to describe an inn, he says so; he simply tells his readers to consult a guidebook. And when he eventually arrives in Rome, and Lector wants him finally to get serious and describe the magnificent city, Belloc refuses: "I am on the threshold of a great experience; I would rather be alone. Good-bye, my readers; good-bye, the world" (444). He leaves us with his benediction and a hastily written bit of verse celebrating his herculean march. The last words of the book are:

*Lector.* But this is dogg—
*Auctor.* Not a word!      (448)

Belloc earned the last word, for at the height of his powers he had written a new kind of travel book, full of cheerful and open laughter. From the mountaintops he could see eternity, but he had no desire to leave the beautiful Earth; he was having far too good a time. As a very old man, Belloc commented that he was "very glad" he walked to Rome.[6]

The critical reaction to *The Path to Rome* was almost overwhelmingly positive. G. K. Chesterton, who admittedly was Belloc's friend, wrote that the book "is the product of the actual and genuine buoyancy and thoughtlessness of a rich intellect" and applauded its "flaming and reverberating folly."[7] C. F. G. Masterman wrote that Belloc would now join that select group of writers whose work excites "an almost personal affection."[8] This comment perhaps comes closest to defining the greatness of the book: it captures the essence of Belloc at the most appealing time of his life.

### The Four Men

Belloc took five years to write *The Four Men* (1912), an extraordinarily long time for him. During its composition he had tentatively titled it *The County of Sussex*; it was to be a straightforward travel narrative.[9] But during the years he spent working on it he suffered two severe disappointments: his disillusioning experience in Parliament and his experience with the *Morning Post*, the journal that he felt exploited and humiliated him. These professional setbacks, plus the fact that as a middle-aged man Belloc was beginning to realize his mortality, changed the direction *The Four Men* was to take.

The Preface suggests that the book will be a companion piece to *The Path to Rome*: it will chronicle a walking tour across land that is sacred to Belloc, this time his home county of Sussex, in the south of England. The impetus for this walk was the author's realization that the forces of time ravage not only man, but the earth as well. In order to reestablish a communion with Sussex before it became something else, Belloc decided to record the adventures that he and three other men had on a walk through the county.

Staring into the fire while sitting at a Sussex inn on the evening of October 29, 1902, Belloc realizes that he is wasting his life in pursuit of money. He is ignoring the things that are "of moment to men." Belloc's starting point is thus the same as that of Wordsworth, a century earlier, whose sonnet "The World Is Too Much with Us" laments the fact that "Getting and spending, we lay waste our powers." Belloc's realization leads to a decision:

"I will go from this place to my home."
When I had said this the deeper voice of an older man answered:
"And since I am going to that same place, let us journey there together."
I turned round, and I was angry, for there had been no one with me when I had entered upon this reverie, and I had thought myself alone. (5—6)

This passage is the first clue that *The Four Men* is to be radically different from *The Path to Rome*. The old man seems to materialize at Belloc's statement about going home, and says that he is headed for "that same place," even though he obviously does not know where Belloc's home is. What the old man is saying, of course, is that he too is going home; thus Belloc suggests his intention to write an allegorical quest narrative in the guise of a realistic travel book.

This strategy is made clear when the two men agree to walk together through Sussex and therefore decide to exchange introductions. The old man will not divulge his real name because it "tells very little . . ." (8). He happily accepts the name "Grizzlebeard" from the Belloc character, who then dubs himself "Myself." The two men vow to "recover . . . the principal joys of the soul" and to "gather . . . some further company . . . "(9). Early on in their journey they enlist two other travelers: the Sailor and the Poet.

On one level at least, these four characters are like the archetypes in a medieval allegory.[10] Grizzlebeard is the voice of experience and wisdom; the Sailor is the adventurer, the link to the physical universe; and the Poet is the artist whose eyes are turned upward to the heavens. Myself is the narrator of the tale, the one who unifies and encompasses the other three. In fact, Belloc once said that the three are just supernatural beings.[11] But as they walk through Sussex discussing abstract issues of life, the characters refuse to remain simply types. Grizzlebeard has not been able to understand the universe or achieve real happiness, although he knows that some actions will certainly not lead to happiness. The Sailor has no plans to go to sea, and apparently no desire to, either. And the Poet, for all of his talk about the creative life, is far less skillful with words than either the Sailor or Myself.

In their discussions along the way, the four show themselves to be evocative and individual characters. For instance, sitting before a fire one night they agree to tell about their first loves. Grizzlebeard's story is simultaneously moving and humorous. He describes how as a young man he fell in love with a woman much older than himself. An accident of fortune called him away for nineteen months, after which he returned to find that she had married a worthy politician and manufacturer of "rectified lard": "'I saw reality all bare, original, evil and instinct with death'" (219). When she and her new husband received Grizzlebeard, he noticed that her skin "'was mottled with patches of dead-white...[her] teeth were various . . . ; her voice was set at a pitch which was not musical; her gestures were sometimes vulgar; her conversation was inane'" (220−21). But the vision of the woman when he loved her stays with him to this day: "'Not even in death, I think, shall I lose her'" (222). Not wanting to end on that potentially sentimental note, Grizzlebeard pours out his mug of beer into the sand, as "'a symbol of what befalls the chief experience in the life of every man'" (223−24).

The Sailor, the next storyteller, starts to describe a woman from Lisbon, then corrects himself: the Lisbon woman was his second love. The first love was the woman from Newhaven. No, *she* was the second, the first was the one from Erith. This goes on until he has named his fourth first love, at which point the others shout him down for being unable to take the storytelling seriously.

The Poet's story is in the tradition of the best Bellocian farce. The Poet once saw a young woman from a distance, across a lake: "'I made at once to watch her form as it passed into the boughs of that lakeside and made in the tracery of them a sort of cloud, as I thought, so that I was not certain for a moment whether I had really seen a human thing or no'" (227).

The Sailor interrupts this reverie and accuses the Poet of telling a "literary lie," one that he either got from a book or intends to put in one. But the Poet is determined to prove the existence of his dream vision, so he begins to recite the five lines that "enshrine her memory":

> "The colour of the morning sky
> Was like a shield of bronze
> The something or other was something or other."

"The what?" said the Sailor. (229)

The Poet proceeds to explain that although he has forgotten the exact words, he remembers the rhythm well enough.

Myself, the final storyteller, holds up a gold coin, to which he has been "'absolutely faithful. . . . Gentlemen, to be faithful in that sort is a rare and a worthy thing!'" (232) He then raises his tankard and finishes his beer, "'for a symbol of what jolly satisfaction a man may get if he will do what every man should do; that is, take life and its ladies as he finds them during his little passage through the daylight, and his limping across the stage of this world'" (232). Myself's symbolic action thus complements Grizzlebeard's. In his discussion of first loves, then, Belloc shows an amazing range of viewpoints, and he keeps them under firm artistic control: the two humorous responses—the Sailor's and the Poet's—are enclosed within the two serious ones. All together, the four responses constitute a subtle panorama that is all the more impressive because it does not insist on a single acceptable statement.

Like many writers, Belloc had no interest in "explaining" his fiction by answering the many questions about the exact meaning of his allegorical characters. His reply was casual: the book had taken so many years to write that the characters had "turned inside out."[12] Raymond Las Vergnas also responded by deflecting the questions:

The most original, and most moving utterance of *The Four Men* does not consist in the historical monologues of Myself, nor of the theories exchanged between Grizzlebeard and the Poet: it comes from the inarticulate, unescapable, imperious chanting of the soil's very soul. Hymns of death and of hope breathe upwards through the yellowing leaves that no wind stirs.[13]

Hymns of death are all around the travelers as they march across Sussex. Even the beauty of the late autumn foretells the coming of winter: "The sky was already of an apple green to the westward, and in the eastern blue there were stars. There also shone what had not yet appeared upon that windless day, a few small wintry clouds, neat and defined in heaven. Above them the moon, past her first quarter but not yet full, was no longer pale, but began to make a cold glory . . ." (104−105). And when the four men separate at the end of their four days' march, Myself notices that the earth embraced them: "I watched them, straining my sad eyes, but in a moment the mist received them and they had disappeared" (303). He remembers, "with a pang that catches men at the clang of bells," that it is November 2, the Day of the Dead.

But if the earth forces man to face his own mortality, it also offers to him something akin to immortality, as Myself phrases it in a final poem that includes the following stanza:

> "He does not die that can bequeath
> Some influence to the land he knows,
> Or dares, persistent, interwreath
> Love permanent with the wild hedgerows;
>   He does not die, but still remains
>   Substantiate with his darling plains."                    (309)

If man can become part of the earth, "it will be a friend for ever, and he has outflanked Death in a way" (309).

In choosing to conclude the book with Myself's poem, Belloc suggests another way to outflank death: through art. The artist figure in *The Four Men* is not the Poet, who is merely a dreamer, but Myself, who feels the need to translate his thoughts into poetry: "I knew . . . that verse would satisfy something at least . . ." (307). Putting his pencil to the paper, Myself pauses, for not considering himself an artist he is filled with self-doubt: "But I would not long hesitate in this manner, for I knew that all creation must be chaos first, and then gestures in the void before it can cast out the completed thing" (308). After having written his poem, Myself characterizes himself as "greatly relieved by . . . the . . . metrical expression" of his thoughts.

The four-stanza poem suggests the basic difference between *The Four Men* and *The Path to Rome*. The earlier book ended with doggerel that Belloc scribbled down while sitting in a cafe in Rome, waiting for his bread and wine. Belloc had no desire to conclude with serious poetry, for his thoughts were focused on the land and the sky, the simple joys of the earth and the salvation of the heavens. But *The Four Men*, like Wordsworth's "The World Is Too Much with Us," describes a pagan, not a Christian salvation. For this reason, the four characters, especially Myself after the others have been enclosed within the mist, are forever looking downward, trying to find in the earth the answers to the questions posed by man's realization of his mortality. When they look at the sky, they see only the bright, blank moon, beautiful but meaningless. The meaning that Myself discovers at the end of the book is partly intellectual, in that he comes to an understanding of the relationship between man and the earth he walks on, and partly aesthetic, for he is able to express that relationship in an artistic shape. He thereby gives his thoughts the permanence that only art affords and exercises the divine powers that few but artists feel.

*The Four Men* is subtitled *A Farrago*, a medley or mixture. Although the four men do sing many songs as they pursue their travels, the book itself is anything but the light-hearted and careless narrative that the word *farrago* implies. *The Path to Rome* is a true farrago; *The Four Men*, as biographer Speaight remarks, is closer in spirit to a fugue. [14]

The melancholy, autumnal spirit of the book was described as early as 1916, when Mandell and Shanks published the first book-length study of Belloc. The authors called it his "old book," and contrasted it with *The Path to Rome*, his "young book." [15] As they did when writing about the earlier travel book, most commentators focused on the extent to which *The Four Men* reflected and defined its author's current state of mind. One critic called it a "microcosm of Belloc's entire outlook." [16] Robert Speaight wrote that the philosophy expressed in the book was to predominate in Belloc as he grew older. [17] This comment suggests the central irony in Belloc's work: the melancholy paganism of his fiction opposes the Catholic polemicism of his nonfiction. But for most readers, who expected a sequel to *The Path to Rome*, Raymond Las Vergnas provided the crucial comment: *The Four Men* "makes no attempt . . . to win the reader's sympathy."[18]

### The Cruise of the "Nona"

Near the end of *The Four Men* Grizzlebeard offers his final piece of advice to Myself: ". . . consider chiefly from now onward those permanent things which are, as it were, the shores of this age and the harbours of our glittering and pleasant but dangerous and wholly changeful sea" (303). When he wrote those words, Belloc did not know just how dangerous and changeful the seas could be. Thirteen years later, for *The Cruise of the "Nona"* (1925), he chose the sea as his subject and central metaphor.

In 1914 Belloc and his good friend Phil Kershaw took a sailing trip along the south and west coasts of England in Belloc's boat, the *Nona*. Although the book would suggest that the two men, plus an occasional local sailor, were at sea some three months, in fact the cruise was interrupted several times while he or Kershaw had to attend to business at home or in London. At one point, Belloc had the *Nona* transported along the coast so that they could resume their cruise in a harbor more to their liking.[19] So *The Cruise of the "Nona"* is like *The Path to Rome* in that Belloc did indeed make the trip, but it is like *The Four Men* in that it is an artistic re-creation.

Some three months before the cruise, Belloc's wife, Elodie, died, leaving him in a profound state of despair. One of the first things he did after her death was travel to Rome, a trip which enabled him to regain contact with the soul of the Catholic world and, perhaps, with the younger Hilaire Belloc who had made the famous pilgrimage there some thirteen years earlier. The trip on the *Nona* had a different kind of therapeutic value: by isolating him, physically, from his hectic daily existence, it allowed him some uninterrupted time to confront his grief and try to conquer it. Sailing his thirty-foot boat along the coast gave him time to smoke his pipe and think. Phil Kershaw was there for him to talk to when he wanted conversation, but mostly Belloc was alone on deck, busying himself with the details of sailing when the wind was up, sitting placidly when the sea was calm.

How much of the book was written during or immediately after the cruise and how much within the next decade is unknown, but it was not published until 1925. The intervening decade gives the book an unusual back-and-forth movement as Belloc alternates between vivid descriptions of the art of sailing and retrospective analyses of the major events of the period. For instance, he is describing how his thoughts were troubled one day on the cruise when he learned of the assassination of Archduke Francis Ferdinand. Like most Englishmen, he was anxious about its implications. He describes looking out toward the distant sea:

Like ghosts, like things themselves made of mist, there passed . . . a procession of great forms, all in line, hastening eastward. It was the Fleet recalled.

The slight haze along the distant water had thickened, perhaps, imperceptibly; or perhaps the great speed of the men-of-war buried them too quickly in the distance. But, from whatever cause, this marvel was of short duration. It was seen for a moment, and in a moment it was gone.

Then I knew that war would come, and my mind was changed. (142)

The eerie combination of this instant and the reverberating and terrible consequences of the war—for the world and for Belloc—gives this passage and others like it its power.

In addition to switching from the present to the past, Belloc switches easily from one subject to another. Like *The Path to Rome* and *The Four Men*, this book is a collection of digressions on the author's favorite subjects. In the Dedication he describes his purpose as "writing down . . . some poor scraps of judgment and memory . . ." (xii). So he discusses the nature and function of literature, the corruption of Parliament, the impossibility of achieving a democracy, and, above all, the need to return to Catholicism. At one point he defines the relationship between the narrative and the digressions by declaring "these musing passages . . . the only ones of real import . . ." in the book (236). Belloc was certainly right to de-emphasize the narrative passages; although many of them are powerful and interesting, the heart of the book is the play of his mind at this difficult point in his life.

Occasionally, the comic spirit manages to bubble to the surface. A discussion of types of modern fools, for example, culminates in this portrait:

> I knew one Fool Secretary of State who . . . used to look at his official documents with a sort of tragic stare, as men look on the dead, and slowly wag them up and down . . . with a hopeless gesture. Then . . . his permanent official . . . would explain to him what they meant, whereupon he would use one after another of the great Fool Phrases . . . such as, "Yes," "I see," "Quite," "Precisely," and then again "Yes." Having done this, he would sign his name . . . and with a groan . . . go off to spend his hundred pounds a week at Brighton. (34)

Belloc's good spirits find perhaps their most successful expression when he creates one of his rhetorical flourishes, reminiscent of some of the Auctor-Lector debates in *The Path to Rome*. Here his subject is the dreariness of his own book, which he calls "already so long as to have become intolerable to the reader, the writer, the printer, and all other concerned in its production, already so heavy as to have become a business to the publisher, the carman, and the railway people . . ." (247).

But the anger and bitterness behind the portrait of the Secretary of State provide a somber counterbalance to Belloc's characteristic sense of humor. Later in *The Cruise of the "Nona,"* for instance, he returns to the subject of "the cancer called Parliament," and writes that some countries "are already rid of it: all are disgusted with it; most will probably have cut it out within a generation" (267). Belloc's great disappointment after having been denied a fellowship, some thirty years earlier, gives rise to a discussion of "the powerful force urging dons to make fools of themselves . . ." (76).

The predominant tone of this book, however, is neither gaiety nor anger, but sadness and resignation. These notes are sounded as early as the Dedication, which concludes with these words: "I am now off to sail the English seas again, and to pursue from thought to thought and from memory to memory such things as have occupied one human soul, and of these some will be of profit to one man and some to another, and most, I suppose, to none at all" (xiv). The most telling phrase in this sentence is the casual "I suppose," for it suggests

Belloc's mental fatigue. He feels no fury or bitterness or scorn, only weariness. In another passage in the book Belloc refers to his "short but too long life" (42). One incident he recounts took place "in the year 1897, before the gods had left this broken world" (61). Or again, when discussing a violent storm during which he feared they might drown, he talks about "this detestable little world which can be so beautiful when it likes" (7). Like the universe in Thomas Hardy's "Hap," Belloc's world could be a heaven or a hell, and it changed from one to another on a whim.

Belloc's devout Catholicism would not allow him to think of life as a cruel and painful game; instead, his faith forced him to try to envision fortune as the expression of the divine will. So he talks often in *The Cruise of the "Nona"* of man's inability to define his own course in life, of his subservience to the force he cannot understand. In concluding the book, Belloc links the sea with the heavens:

The sea is the matrix of creation, and we have the memory of it in our blood. . . . But far more than this is there in the sea. It presents, upon the greatest scale we mortals can bear, those not mortal powers which brought us into being. It is not only the symbol or the mirror, but especially is it the messenger of the Divine. (328)

The sea is the "common sacrament of this world" (329).

With passages like this, Belloc defined his attempt to understand his recent personal tragedy. But an earlier discussion of the divine provides a more accurate picture of his state of mind. He is describing how every child can see the divine in all of the beautiful things of this world, "but with the passage of time they are lost altogether. The light in the lantern goes out, and the living thing within us fails, and is stupefied, and dies" (28). Even the divine could offer Belloc no escape from the tyranny of time.

The critical reception of *The Cruise of the "Nona"* was positive, although, as usual, the reviewers saw very different things in the book. The *Times Literary Supplement* wrote that "there seems to blow through his pages a breeze as inspiring as those he met with in the Nona."[20] Leonard Woolf, on the other hand, said that it "leaves one with a bitter, dusty, gritty taste in the mouth."[21]

In his comic introduction to *The Footpath Way: An Anthology for Walkers* Belloc had written, "Remember that of the many ways of walking there is one way which is the greatest of all, and that is to walk away" (15). Fourteen years after this quip, Belloc completed his book about walking away.

## Chapter Eight

# Conclusion

Few writers offered their opinions as often and as forcefully as Hilaire Belloc did, yet few writers revealed less about themselves. The split between his ferocious public personality and his essential self was dramatic. A leading man of letters in the first quarter of the century, Belloc today remains a mystery.

He was, first, an active political and economic radical. With his pamphlets and novels, his speeches, and his service in Parliament, Belloc attempted to warn his fellow citizens that they were becoming enslaved by the money powers—the banks, the industries, the newspapers—and, most of all, by their Parliament. The great heritage of representative democracy, he asserted, was a cruel facade, a means by which the party leaders maintained their own power, salary, and perquisites—and effectively thwarted the will of the nation. When a series of public improprieties and scandals gave credence to his argument, people listened. Yet when he was asked for a solution, he could offer only general proposals for electoral reform or, to the alarm of many, a plea for a revival of the strong monarchy. While Europe was witnessing the ascent of Mussolini and then Hitler, Belloc argued that only one-man rule could protect the rights of the common citizen against the money powers.

Belloc's most substantial historical work—his series of studies of monarchy, especially the English crown—was an attempt to validate his theories of contemporary politics and economics. The reading public enjoyed his histories because of their vitality and drama. His saga of the tragic debacle of Henry VIII's split from Rome, and the resulting birth of the aristocracy which destroyed the monarchy, was vigorous reading. But in addressing the general reader he ignored the scholar. Without proper documentation his books failed in their chief purpose: to refute the work of the "official Whig historians." Belloc was dismissed as a brilliant but unreliable publicist.

Despite his active involvement in the issues of the day, Belloc was essentially an artist. The descriptive powers that animated his better histories found their natural outlet in his essays, travel books, and poetry. Belloc was one of the great masters of English prose, and his essays provide the best overview of his many interests and moods. Written in an allusive and informal style dictated by his frantic pace, the essays range from inspired nonsense about trivialities to prose poems on death. His three outstanding travel books record his odyssey from effervescence to despair.

Belloc's best and most permanent work is his poetry. His concept of poetry—as well as of all the arts—was purely classical. Like his near contemporary, A. E. Housman, he slowly and carefully shaped his experience into the rigorous patterns established by the masters of Western prosody. He achieved what the greatest classical poets have always achieved: a slim body of ordered and precise celebrations of love and meditations on death. In his best poems he transformed his own passions and despair into cool and impersonal evocations of pure emotion. As a strict classicist in an age of artistic experimentation and upheaval, Belloc was as radical in aesthetics as he was in politics.

The great irony of Belloc's literary career is that his vision of the world was essentially similar to that of the writers he scorned. Modern culture was for Belloc the same wasteland it was for Eliot. The modern writers, especially the poets, attempted to fashion a literature that would trace accurately the pulse of modern existence. Belloc, however, believed that the basic human condition is changeless, and that therefore the artist's responsibility is to create timeless works of art from the raw materials of contemporary life. Only by imposing the acknowledged standards of artistic achievement, he believed, could the chaos of modern life be transcended. Thus, while James Joyce was writing a modern epic patterned on the story of Ulysses, Belloc preferred to stay with the original Greek poem.

Although Belloc's isolation from the progressive literary activity of his own day can be explained by his aesthetic principles, it is consistent as well with the entire development of his character. His story is fundamentally a search for a homeland and security. When he was just weeks old, his family fled from the approaching Prussian troops. His father died when the boy was an infant. He grew up English, and his awkward year as a French soldier—when his accent isolated him from the other soldiers—was in many ways a disappointment. Back in England and attempting a political career, he was branded a Frenchman. His only period of security, the Oxford years, had been ruined when the university denied him the fellowship he desired.

Without the steady income or the time needed to become a scholar, he was forced to live by his pen. He wrote as quickly as he could, rarely allowing himself the luxury of revision. The Oxford disappointment became an obsession. When personal losses taught him the fragility of the world, he headed for his only safe port, Catholicism. His histories became biased and distorted as he tried to resurrect what he saw as the orderly and changeless world of the Middle Ages, when citizens owned property and loved God. By age fifty he had become a Catholic apologist whose main audience was his fellow Catholics.

Catholicism was for Belloc a coherent system of belief whose main appeal was its permanence. Everything that was touched by mortality was taken from him. He was left without the influence he once had, and without his wife and the two sons whom disease and the two wars had claimed. All that remained was his faith.

But he wrote as long as he could. His greatness is obscured because he was a professional writer or, to use the term he often used to describe himself, a hack. Had circumstances been otherwise, had he written just fifteen books instead of ten times that number, his achievement would be easier to discern. But fame is often harsh with those who write for a living. It is both pleasing and sad to think of what Belloc might have done had he been able to exercise his prodigious talents more selectively. What he produced, however, is considerable: several dozen masterful lyrics, a handful of exciting histories, dozens of sparkling essays, three distinguished novels, and three triumphant travel books. For all his bluster, prejudice, and self-delusion, he created a formidable body of first-class literature. A man who was disappointed so many times by the world, he realized at least his early wish: to make a name for himself in English letters.

# Notes and References

*Chapter One*

1. Robert Speaight, *The Life of Hilaire Belloc* (London, 1957), p. 6.
2. Marie Belloc Lowndes, *"I, Too, Have Lived in Arcadia,"* (New York, 1942), p. 97.
3. J. B. Morton, *Hilaire Belloc: A Memoir* (London, 1955), p. 3.
4. Speaight, p. 5.
5. Morton, p. 3.
6. Lowndes, *Arcadia*, p. 48.
7. Speaight, p. 7.
8. Ibid.
9. Lowndes, *Arcadia*, p. 137.
10. Speaight, pp. 7−8.
11. Ibid., p. 9.
12. Marie Belloc Lowndes, *The Young Hilaire Belloc: Some Records of Youth and Middle Age* (New York, 1956), p. 35.
13. Speaight, p. 13.
14. Ibid., p. 15.
15. See, for example, the letter reprinted in Speaight, pp. 28−29.
16. Lowndes, *Young Belloc*, p. 86.
17. Speaight, p. 34.
18. Ibid.
19. Lowndes, *Young Belloc*, p. 88.
20. Ibid., p. 93.
21. Ibid., p. 92.
22. Speaight, p. 38.
23. Ibid., p. 39.
24. Ibid.
25. Ibid., p. 40.
26. Ibid., p. 41.
27. Ibid., pp. 45−46.
28. Lowndes, *Young Belloc*, p. 97.
29. Speaight, p. 57.
30. Ibid.
31. Lowndes, *Young Belloc*, p. 100.

32. Speaight, p. 57.
33. Lowndes, *Young Belloc*, p. 102.
34. Speaight, p. 73.
35. Lowndes, *Young Belloc*, p. 123.
36. Speaight, pp. 77, 84.
37. Ibid., pp. 89–90.
38. Ibid., p. 95.
39. Ibid., p. 98.
40. Hilaire Belloc, *Letters from Hilaire Belloc*, ed. Robert Speaight (London, 1958), p. 238.
41. Speaight, p. 99.
42. Ibid., p. 101.
43. Lowndes, *Young Belloc*, p. 134.
44. Speaight, p. 113.
45. Belloc, *Letters*, p. 124.
46. Speaight, p. 119.
47. Ibid., p. 122.
48. Belloc, *Letters*, p. 260.
49. Speaight, p. 122.
50. Ibid., p. 121.
51. Ibid., p. 156.
52. Ibid., p. 191.
53. Ibid., p. 193.
54. Ibid., p. 203.
55. Ibid., p. 204.
56. Ibid., p. 214.
57. Ibid., p. 217.
58. Ibid., pp. 217–18.
59. Ibid., p. 218.
60. Ibid., p. 219.
61. Ibid., p. 243.
62. Ibid., p. 244.
63. Ibid., p. 255.
64. Ibid., p. 265.
65. Ibid.
66. Ibid., p. 258.
67. Belloc, *Letters*, p. 27.
68. Speaight, p. 282.
69. Ibid., p. 293.
70. Ibid., p. 310.

71. Ibid., p. 313.
72. Ibid., p. 330.
73. Ibid., p. 344.
74. Ibid., p. 348, 355.
75. Ibid., p. 371.
76. Ibid., p. 372.
77. Ibid., p. 530.
78. Belloc, *Letters*, p. 248.
79. Ibid., p. 207.
80. Ibid., p. 177.
81. Ibid., p. 190.
82. Ibid., p. 246.
83. Ibid., p. 286.

*Chapter Two*

1. Garry Wills, *Chesterton: Man and Mask* (New York, 1961), p. 46.
2. Eleanor and Reginald Jebb, *Testimony to Hilaire Belloc* (London, 1956), p. 20.
3. Edward Lear, "There Was an Old Man with a Beard," in Iona and Peter Opie, eds., *The Oxford Book of Children's Verse* (New York: Oxford University Press, 1933), p. 183.
4. Lewis Carroll, "Jabberwocky," in *The Oxford Book of Children's Verse*, p. 241.
5. Hilaire Belloc, *The Cruise of the "Nona"* (London, 1925), p. 79.
6. This and all subsequent citations of Belloc's poetry refer to *Complete Verse* (London, 1970), which does not reproduce the illustrations of the volumes of light verse. *Cautionary Verses* (several different editions), which includes all of the light verse except *The Modern Traveller* (London: Edward Arnold, 1898), reproduces the illustrations.
7. Speaight, pp. 112, 114.
8. Ibid., p. 115.
9. Ibid., p. 116.
10. Ibid., p. 270.
11. *New Yorker*, August 30, 1941, p. 56.
12. Hilaire Belloc, *Milton* (London, 1935), p. 219.
13. Ibid., p. 128.
14. Hilaire Belloc, "Preface to *First and Second Poems*" by Ruth Pitter (London: Sheed and Ward, 1927), reprinted in J. A. De Chantigny, ed., *Hilaire Belloc's Prefaces: Written for Fellow Authors* (Chicago: 1971), p. 213.

15. Belloc, *Letters*, p. 285.

16. Belloc, *The Cruise of the "Nona,"* p. 27.

17. Belloc, *Letters*, p. 294.

18. Belloc, *Milton*, p. 57.

19. Hilaire Belloc, *Avril* (London: Duckworth, 1904), p. 179.

20. Ibid., p. 200.

21. Belloc, *Milton*, pp. 31, 32.

22. Ibid., p. 211.

23. W. H. Auden, "In Memory of W.B. Yeats," in *The Collected Poems of W. H. Auden* (New York: Random House, 1945), p. 50.

24. *Times* (London), December 22, 1910, p. 519.

25. Speaight, p. 512.

26. Ibid., p. 342.

27. *Saturday Review*, November 10, 1923, pp. 523–24.

28. *New York Times*, December 2, 1923, p. 8, Sec. III.

29. Belloc, *Letters*, p. 223.

30. *Catholic World*, August, 1939, p. 633.

31. *Times* (London), May 28, 1938, p. 375.

32. George Sampson, *The Concise Cambridge History of English Literature* (Cambridge: At the University Press, 1941), p. 1012.

33. Belloc, *Letters*, p. 223.

*Chapter Three*

1. Hilaire Belloc, "On the Decline of the Book," in *First and Last*, 5th ed. (London, 1927), p. 130.

2. Hilaire Belloc, *Marie Antoinette* (London, 1909), p. 402.

3. Hilaire Belloc, "On Footnotes," in *On* (London, 1923; reprint ed., Freeport, N.Y., 1967), p. 47.

4. Hilaire Belloc, *Robespierre* (New York, 1901), p. ix.

5. Hilaire Belloc, "On Macaulay," in *A Conversation with an Angel* (New York, 1929), p. 209.

6. See, for example, "On Macaulay" (p. 206): "God knows he lied freely!"

7. *Nation and Athenaeum*, May 19, 1928, p. 210.

8. Speaight, p. 271.

9. Ibid., p. 272.

10. Ibid., p. 323.

11. Ibid.

12. The English edition of this book has a different title and publisher:

*The Last Days of the French Monarchy* (London: Chapman and Hall, 1916).

13. *Nation*, January 6, 1910, p. 13.

14. Belloc, *Letters*, p. 74.

15. Speaight, pp. 426–27.

16. Ibid., p. 424.

17. Quoted ibid., p. 372.

18. Citations refer to the American edition: *Louis XIV* (New York: Harper and Brothers, 1938).

19. The English edition of this book has a different title and publisher: *The Last Rally* (London: Cassell and Co., 1940).

20. *Outlook*, October 17, 1928, p. 994.

21. Albert Leon Guerard, "Danton," *New York Herald Tribune, Books*, April 1, 1928, p. 16.

*Chapter Four*

1. The Dutton edition also contains Belloc's other academic satire, *Caliban's Guide to Letters*. *Lambkin's Remains* was originally published by the Proprietors of the *J. C. R.* in Oxford, 1900. *Caliban's Guide to Letters* was originally published by Duckworth and Co., London, 1903.

2. Speaight, p. 122.

3. *Times* (London), September 30, 1904, p. 297.

4. Ibid., July 16, 1908, p. 230.

5. *Spectator*, June 4, 1932, p. 810.

6. *Times* (London), May 26, 1932, p. 386.

7. Ibid., May 11, 1911, p. 186.

8. Speaight, p. 500.

9. Ibid.

10. *Saturday Review*, July 6, 1929, p. 1165.

11. Ibid., May 27, 1922, p. 555.

12. *Times* (London), May 11, 1922, p. 306.

13. *Spectator*, July 30, 1927, p. 193.

14. Belloc, "Preface to *Week-End Wodehouse*" (London: Herbert Jenkins, n.d.), reprinted in Chantigny, ed., *Hilaire Belloc's Prefaces* (Chicago, 1971), p. 342.

*Chapter Five*

1. Hilaire Belloc, "A Conversation with a Reader," in *Short Talks with the Dead* (London, 1926; reprint ed., Freeport, N.Y., 1967), p. 108. Citations refer to the reprint edition.

2. Ibid., p. 112.

3. There are several major exceptions, such as *Many Cities* (1928) and Places (1942). Belloc also wrote whole collections of essays on the subject of Catholicism. In addition, he sometimes re-collected essays, as in the case of *On Sailing the Sea* (London: Methuen and Co., 1939).

4. The one major exception is "On Translation," which was published separately by Oxford's Clarendon Press (1931) and later included in several of Belloc's collections and re-collections.

5. Hilaire Belloc, "On Cheeses," in *First and Last*, 3d ed. (London, 1924), p. 7.

6. Ibid., p. 8.

7. Hilaire Belloc, *Hills and the Sea* (1906; reprint ed., Westport, Conn.: Greenwood Press, 1970). Citations refer to the reprint edition.

8. Hilaire Belloc, "On Books," in *The Silence of the Sea* (New York: Sheed and Ward, 1940), p. 140.

9. *Times* (London), May 27, 1926, p. 351.

10. *New York Times*, December 27, 1931, *Book Review*, p. 2.


*Chapter Six*

1. Speaight, p. 296.

2. *Saturday Review*, March 25, 1911, p. 357.

3. *Times* (London), December 30, 1920, p. 883.

4. Belloc was instrumental in forming the Distributist League. See Speaight, p. 485.

5. Hilaire Belloc, *The Servile State* (London, 1912; 3d ed., London, 1927). Citations refer to the third edition.

6. Speaight, p. 316.

7. The Preface to the second edition is reprinted in the third edition. The quotation cited appears on p. *x*.

8. Citations refer to the American edition, *The Restoration of Property* (New York, 1936).

9. E. M. W. Tillyard, "Mr. Belloc's Milton," *Spectator* 154 (April 5, 1935): 576.

10. For example, the first sentence of John P. McCarthy's *Hilaire Belloc: Edwardian Radical* (Indianapolis, 1978) reads, "Hilaire Belloc is chiefly known as a neomedievalist essayist-poet and Catholic apologetic historian, whose claim to admiration by our generation is compromised by his sympathy for authoritarianism and his anti-Semitism."

11. Speaight, p. 474.

12. Belloc, *Letters*, p. 116.

13. The text of *The Jews* offers no reasons to distrust Belloc's sincerity in this preface. The situation here does not parallel that in *The Servile State*.

14. Speaight, p. 454.

15. *New York Times*, March 28, 1922, pp. 14, 20.

16. Speaight, pp. 346–47.

17. *Times* (London), March 30, 1922, p. 203.

18. David Lodge, "Chesterbelloc and the Jews," in *The Novelist at the Crossroads* (Ithaca, N.Y.: Cornell University Press, 1971), p. 154.

19. *New York Times*, July 24, 1927, *Book Review*, p. 1.

20. "A Notable Controversy," *New Statesman* 27 (November 27, 1926): 202.

21. "Wells Versus Belloc," *New York Herald Tribune, Books*, January 2, 1927, p. 15.

22. Raymond Las Vergnas, *Chesterton, Belloc, Baring*, trans. C. C. Martindale, S.J., (London, 1938), p. 70.

*Chapter Seven*

1. Jebb and Jebb, p. 35.

2. Belloc, *Letters*, p. 129.

3. Speaight, p. 81.

4. *The Footpath Way* (London: Sidgwick and Jackson, 1911).

5. Jebb and Jebb, p. 38.

6. Speaight, p. 164.

7. Ibid., p. 161.

8: Ibid., pp. 162–63.

9. Ibid., p. 325.

10. See, for example, Frederick Wilhelmsen's *Hilaire Belloc: No Alienated Man* (New York, 1953), p. 11.

11. Speaight, p. 325.

12. Ibid.

13. Las Vergnas, p. 78.

14. Speaight, p. 326.

15. C. Creighton Mandell and Edward Shanks, *Hilaire Belloc: The Man and His Work* (London, 1916), p. 135.

16. Robert Hamilton, *Hilaire Belloc* (London, 1945), p. 37.

17. Speaight, p. 327.

18. Las Vergnas, p. 76.

19. Speaight, p. 346.

20. *Times* (London), May 7, 1925, p. 312.

21. Leonard Woolf, *"The Cruise of the Nona,"* *Nation and Athenaeum* (May 16, 1925), p. 207.

# Selected Bibliography

## PRIMARY SOURCES

Following is a partial list of Belloc's writings. Most of his books have a long and complicated bibliographical history, with a number of different English and American editions. This selected bibliography lists only the first English editions except when I have quoted from other editions.

### 1. Poetry

*The Bad Child's Book of Beasts.* Oxford: Alden and Co., 1896.
*Cautionary Tales for Children.* London: Eveleigh Nash, 1907.
*Ladies and Gentlemen.* London: Duckworth, 1932.
*The Modern Traveller.* London: Edward Arnold, 1898.
*A Moral Alphabet.* London: Edward Arnold, 1899.
*More Beasts (for Worse Children).* London: Edward Arnold, 1897.
*More Peers.* London: Stephen Swift, 1911.
*New Cautionary Tales.* London: Duckworth, 1930.
*Sonnets and Verse.* London: Duckworth, 1923.
*Sonnets and Verse.* London: Duckworth, 1938.
*Verses.* London: Duckworth, 1910.
*Verses and Sonnets.* London: Ward and Downey, 1896.

### 2. Travel and Topography

*The Contrast.* London: J. W. Arrowsmith, 1923.
*The Cruise of the "Nona."* London: Constable and Co., 1925. Reprint. Boston: Houghton Mifflin Company, 1925.
*Esto Perpetua.* London: Duckworth, 1906.
*The Four Men.* London: Thomas Nelson and Sons, 1912.
*The Path to Rome.* London: George Allen, 1902. Reprint. New York: G. P. Putnam's Sons, 1902.
*The Pyrenees.* London: Methuen and Co., 1909.
*The River of London.* London: T. N. Foulis, 1912.
*Sussex.* London: Adam and Charles Black, 1906.

3. Essays

*A Conversation with an Angel.* London: Jonathan Cape, 1928. Reprint.
    New York: Harper and Brothers, 1929.
*A Conversation with a Cat.* London: Cassell and Co., 1931. Reprint. New
    York: Harper and Brothers, 1931.
*First and Last.* 5th ed. London: Methuen and Co., 1927.
*Hills and the Sea.* London: Methuen and Co., 1906. Reprint. Westport,
    Conn.: Greenwood Press, 1970.
*On.* London: Methuen and Co., 1923. Reprint. Freeport, N.Y.: Books
    for Libraries Press, 1967.
*On Anything.* London: Constable and Co., 1910.
*On Everything.* London: Methuen and Co., 1909.
*On Nothing.* London: Methuen and Co., 1908.
*On Something.* London: Methuen and Co., 1910. Reprint. New York:
    E. P. Dutton and Co., 1911.
*One Thing and Another.* London: Hollis and Carter, 1955.
*Short Talks with the Dead.* London: The Cayme Press, 1926. Reprint.
    Freeport, N.Y.: Books for Libraries Press, 1967.
*The Silence of the Sea.* London: Cassell and Co., 1941.
*This and That.* London: Methuen and Co., 1912.

4. Fiction

*Belinda.* London: Constable and Co., 1928. Reprint. New York: Harper
    and Brothers, 1929.
*But Soft—We are Observed.* London: Arrowsmith, 1928.
*Caliban's Guide to Letters.* London: Duckworth, 1903. Reprint. New York:
    E. P. Dutton and Co., 1903.
*A Change in the Cabinet.* London: Methuen and Co., 1909.
*The Emerald of Catherine the Great.* London: Arrowsmith, 1926.
*Emmanuel Burden.* London: Methuen and Co., 1904.
*The Girondin.* London: Thomas Nelson and Sons, 1911.
*The Green Overcoat.* London: Simpkin, Marshall, Hamilton, Kent and
    Co., 1912.
*The Haunted House.* London: Arrowsmith, 1927. Reprint. New York:
    Harper and Brothers, 1928.
*The Hedge and the Horse.* London: Cassell and Co., 1936.
*Lambkin's Remains.* Oxford: The Proprietors of the J. C. R., 1900. Reprint.
    New York: E. P. Dutton and Co., 1903.
*The Man Who Made Gold.* London: Arrowsmith, 1930.

*The Mercy of Allah.* London: Chatto and Windus, 1922.
*The Missing Masterpiece.* London: Arrowsmith, 1929.
*Mr. Clutterbuck's Election.* London: Eveleigh Nash, 1908.
*Mr. Petre.* London: Arrowsmith, 1925.
*Pongo and the Bull.* London: Constable and Co., 1910.
*The Postmaster-General.* London: Arrowsmith, 1932.


5. Histories

*The Campaign of 1812.* London: Thomas Nelson and Sons, 1924.
*Charles the First.* London: Cassell and Co., 1933. Reprint. Philadelphia:
    J. B. Lippincott Co., 1933.
*Charles II.* New York: Harper and Brothers, 1939. (English edition,
    *The Last Rally.* London: Cassell and Co., 1940.)
*Cranmer.* London: Cassell and Co., 1931.
*Cromwell.* London: Cassell and Co., 1934. Reprint. Philadelphia: J. B.
    Lippincott Co., 1934.
*Danton.* London: James Nisbet and Co., 1899. Reprint. New York:
    Charles Scribner's Sons, 1899.
*Elizabethan Commentary.* London: Cassell and Co., 1942.
*Europe and the Faith.* London: Constable and Co., 1920.
*The Eye-Witness.* London: Eveleigh Nash, 1908.
*The French Revolution.* London: Williams and Norgate, 1911. Reprint.
    New York: Henry Holt and Co., 1911.
*High Lights of the French Revolution.* New York: The Century Co., 1916.
    (English edition, *Last Days of the French Monarchy.* London: Chapman
    and Hale, 1916.)
*A History of England.* Vols. I—IV. London: Methuen and Co., 1925,
    1927, 1928, 1931. Reprint. New York: G. P. Putnam's Sons, 1925,
    1927, 1928, 1931.
*How the Reformation Happened.* London: Jonathan Cape, 1928.
*James the Second.* London: Faber and Gwyer, 1928. Reprint. Philadelphia:
    J. B. Lippincott Co., 1928.
*Joan of Arc.* London: Cassell and Co., 1929.
*Marie Antoinette.* London: Methuen and Co., 1909.
*Milton.* London: Cassell and Co., 1935.
*Miniatures of French History.* London: Thomas Nelson and Sons, 1925.
*Monarchy: A Study of Louis XIV.* London: Cassell and Co., 1938. (American
    edition, *Louis XIV.* New York: Harper and Brothers, 1938.)
*Napoleon.* London: Cassell and Co., 1932.

*Richelieu.* London: Ernest Benn, 1930.

*Robespierre.* London: James Nisbet and Co., 1901. Reprint. New York: Charles Scribner's Sons, 1901.

*Wolsey.* London: Cassell and Co., 1930.

6. Works of Controversy

*A Companion to Mr. Wells's "Outline of History."* London: Sheed and Ward, 1926.

*An Essay on the Nature of Contemporary England.* London: Constable and Co., 1937.

*An Essay on the Restoration of Property.* London: The Distributist League, 1936. Reprint. *The Restoration of Property.* New York: Sheed and Ward, 1936.

*The Free Press.* London: George Allen and Unwin, 1918.

*The House of Commons and Monarchy.* London: George Allen and Unwin, 1920.

*The Jews.* London: Constable and Co., 1922. Reprint. 3d ed. Boston: Houghton Mifflin, 1937.

*Mr. Belloc Still Objects to Mr. Wells's "Outline of History."* London: Sheed and Ward, 1926.

*The Party System* (with Cecil Chesterton). London: Stephen Swift, 1911.

*The Servile State.* London: T. N. Foulis, 1912. Reprint of 3d ed. London: Constable and Co., 1927.

7. Collections and Anthologies

*Belloc: A Biographical Anthology.* Herbert Van Thal and Jane Soames Nickerson, eds. London: George Allen and Unwin, 1970.

*Belloc Essays.* Anthony Foster, ed. London: Methuen, 1955.

*Cautionary Verses.* London: Duckworth, 1940. Collects all of the light verse except *The Modern Traveller.*

*Complete Verse.* London: Gerald Duckworth, 1970. Contains all the verse, but does not include the illustrations for the light verse.

*Hilaire Belloc: An Anthology of his Prose and Verse.* W. N. Roughead, ed. London: R. Hart-Davis, 1951.

*Hilaire Belloc's Prefaces: Written for Fellow Authors.* J. A. Chantigny, ed. Chicago: Loyola University Press, 1971.

*Hilaire Belloc's Stories, Essays, and Poems.* J. B. Morton, ed. London: Dent, 1957.

*Letters from Hilaire Belloc.* Robert Speaight, ed. London: Hollis and Carter, 1958.
*A Picked Company: Being a Selection from the Writings of H. Belloc.* London: Methuen and Co., 1915.
*Selected Essays.* John Edward Dineen, ed. Philadelphia: J. B. Lippincott Co., 1936.


SECONDARY SOURCES

1. Bibliography

**Cahill, Patrick.** *The English First Editions of Hilaire Belloc.* London: n.p., 1953. The authoritative bibliography of Belloc's writing.

2. Books and Parts of Books

**Bergonzi, Bernard.** *The Turn of a Century.* New York: Barnes and Noble Books, 1973. The chapter "Chesterton and/or Belloc" is an analysis of Chesterbelloc and of Belloc's poetry.
**Braybrooke, Patrick.** *Some Catholic Novelists: Their Art and Outlook.* London: Burns Oates and Washbourne, 1931. Chapter entitled "Hilaire Belloc as a Novelist" argues that while his novels are "a holiday" they are often complicated and problematical.
————. *Some Thoughts on Hilaire Belloc.* Philadelphia: J. B. Lippincott Co., 1923. An almost unreadable book, full of unsupported criticism.
**Chesterton, G. K.** *The Autobiography of G. K. Chesterton.* New York: Sheed and Ward, 1936. The chapter "Portrait of a Friend" is a tribute to Belloc.
**Hamilton, Robert.** *Hilaire Belloc: An Introduction to his Spirit and Work.* London: Douglas Organ, 1945. A useful introductory pamphlet undercut by the author's acknowledged inability to evaluate the poetry.
**Haynes, Renee.** *Hilaire Belloc.* London: Longmans, Green and Co., 1953; Writers and Their Work, no. 35. Excellent introductory pamphlet.
**Hynes, Samuel.** *Edwardian Occasions.* New York: Oxford University Press, 1972. The chapter "The Chesterbelloc" is a general essay on Chesterton and Belloc.
**Jebb, Eleanor, and Jebb, Reginald.** *Testimony to Hilaire Belloc.* London: Methuen and Co., 1956. Useful memoir and commentary by daughter and son-in-law.

**Kellogg, Gene.** *The Vital Tradition: The Catholic Novelist in a Period of Convergence.* Chicago: Loyola University Press, 1970. Includes a good analysis of *Emmanuel Burden.*

**Las Vergnas, Raymond.** *Chesterton, Belloc, Baring.* Translated by C. C. Martindale, S. J. London: Sheed and Ward, 1938. Good brief analysis of the prose.

**Lodge, David.** *The Novelist at the Crossroads.* Ithaca, N.Y.: Cornell University Press, 1971. The chapter "Chesterbelloc and the Jews" is the best analysis of the difficult question of Belloc and anti-Semitism.

**Lowndes, Marie Belloc.** *"I, Too, Have Lived in Arcadia."* New York: Dodd, Mead and Co. 1942. Memoir by Belloc's sister provides biographical information about his youth.

————.*The Young Hilaire Belloc: Some Records of Youth and Middle Age.* New York: P. J. Kenedy and Sons, 1956. An expanded memoir of the early Belloc.

**McCarthy, John P.** *Hilaire Belloc: Edwardian Radical.* Indianapolis: Liberty Press, 1978. Full-length study of Belloc's political and economic ideas.

**Mandell, C. Creighton, and Shanks, Edward.** *Hilaire Belloc: The Man and his Work.* London: Methuen and Co., 1916. Written during World War I, this general introduction devotes one third of its pages to Belloc's war journalism.

**Morton, J. B.** *Hilaire Belloc: A Memoir.* London: Hollis and Carter, 1955. Memoir mixed with valuable interpretation by a good friend.

**Reilly, Joseph J.** *Dear Prue's Husband.* New York: The Macmillan Company, 1932. The chapter "The Art of Belloc, Biographer" evaluates Belloc by comparing him to Carlyle, Macaulay, and Froude.

**Speaight, Robert.** *The Life of Hilaire Belloc.* London: Hollis and Carter, 1957. The authorized and authoritative biography. Also provides excellent commentary. The best book on Belloc.

**Swinnerton, Frank.** *The Georgian Literary Scene.* London: J. M. Dent, 1938. Includes commentary on Belloc's prose.

**Wilhelmsen, Frederick.** *Hilaire Belloc: No Alienated Man.* New York: Sheed and Ward, 1953. Argues that Belloc was an "integrated Christian humanist."

**Wells, H. G.** *Mr. Belloc Objects to "The Outline of History."* New York: George H. Doran Co., 1926.

**Wills, Garry.** *Chesterton: Man and Mask.* New York: Sheed and Ward, 1961. Contains the best brief analysis of Belloc.

### 3. Festschrift

**Woodruff, Douglas,** ed. *For Hilaire Belloc: Essays in Honor of His 71st Birthday.* New York: Sheed and Ward, 1947. A collection of essays on history by various friends and scholars.

### 4. Articles

**Bordeaux, André.** "La Personalité d'Hilaire Belloc et sa réputation d'écrivain." *Etudes Anglaises* 11 (1958): 331–37. General assessment of his personality and criticism of Speaight's *Life of Hilaire Belloc.*

**Burdett, Osbert.** "Hilaire Belloc." *London Mercury* 30, no. 175 (May, 1934): 133–42. A competent general appreciation.

**Clery, Arthur E.** "The Philosophy of Sanity: Chesterton and Belloc." *Studies* 11 (1922): 571–81: Relates Belloc to Shaw and Wilde as iconoclasts.

**Jags, David.** "The Stoicism of Hilaire Belloc." *Renascence* 27, no. 2 (Winter, 1975): 89–100. Traces Belloc's stoicism as a complement to his Catholicism.

**Kantra, Robert A.** "Irony in Belloc." *Renascence* 17 (Spring, 1965): 131–36. A brief discussion of Belloc's prose using Frye's definition of irony.

**MacCurtain, Austin.** "The Redeemed Pagan." *Studies* 46 (1957): 207–12. Analyzes the conflict between Belloc's Catholicism and his pagan spirit.

**Madeleva, Sister M.** "Belloc as Biographer." *Bookman* 72 (February, 1931): 607–12. A flattering evaluation of *Marie Antoinette, Richelieu, Joan of Arc,* and *Wolsey* from the perspective of Catholic history.

**Pennington, Richard.** "Hilaire Belloc as Poet." *Bookman* 79 (October, 1930): 22–23. Argues that Belloc will be remembered as a poet.

# Index

(The works of Belloc are listed under his name.)

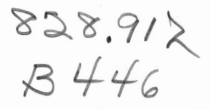